First Printing: 2016

ISBN 978-1-365-57438-2

Lulu Press, Inc.
Raleigh, NC 27607

www.alexmkyte.com

Dedicated to those who labor for the public good

TABLE OF CONTENTS

Chapter 1

INTRODUCTION: CONSENSUS WITHOUT TRUST

On The Cryptographic Enforcement of Distributed Protocols

INTRO

Most services on the internet work by having a lot of servers owned by the same group of people running software that receives input from untrusted clients and use it to craft output for them. In this classic client-server network model, the trust ends at the perimeter of the server farm. The host trusts their own systems, and validates everything from clients against their own state. This type of model is starting to reach growing pains as Moore's law breaks down. As the speed of CPU development slows we see a loss of the ability of the most powerful computers to outpace the request rate of hundreds of thousands of cheaper consumer devices had by clients.

In 1995 an Italian political group called the Strano Network began visiting the websites of the French government quite frequently. So frequently, in fact, that the servers and their network connections were completely monopolized. This was the first distributed denial of service (DDoS). It was only 1995, and the first distributed denial of service had already been carried out. Here we saw that a relatively small number of actors could take down a large, centralized system. Even when the system stays up, hardware can be damaged and server farm contracts can be lost. Non-malicious DDoSes happen all of the time as well, where a small site is linked by a major news organization and suddenly has hundreds of dollars in hosting charges from their provider. In any client-server model, the server is a single point of failure. In response to this, alternate models of computation have been created. We will focus on decentralized and distributed systems.

DECENTRALIZED AND DISTRIBUTED SYSTEMS

A decentralized system removes the single point of failure, typically relying on a number of "supervisor" servers. Sometimes ordinary client servers can be promoted to these roles, but a decentralized system typically places a lot of trust in these supervisors. When a network problem occurs or a node goes down, the trusted nodes will elect a new leader. If one loses enough nodes, a decentralized system can be partitioned into smaller networks that do not synchronize, so it still has failure states. When leaders are lost, complex election algorithms such as Paxos and Raft must be used to safely choose a new leader.

A distributed system is the most egalitarian. Every node in the system is able to both request services and provide services to other nodes. Depending on the amount of bandwidth available to nodes, as well as port availability, some clients may only be consumers. At its core though, a distributed system is characterized by allowing untrusted nodes to carry out services for other nodes.

This brings us to the problem which this book will focus on. How does one create a system which will provide the promised services and properties even if a significantly large minority of the network is untrustworthy? While malicious attackers first come to mind, untrustworthy can refer to sensors which sometimes misbehave and network connections which corrupt or tamper with data during transmission.

By the end of this book, the reader will understand some of the best successes we've had. We will focus on real-life systems such as BitTorrent, Bitcoin, Ethereum, Tor, I2P, Signal, ZeroCash, and others. The reader will also have a grasp of a framework for designing a new system. The hope is that this book may inspire intuition in the reader.

VECTOR CLOCKS AND TIME

Computer time seems reliable until one is working with more than one computer. Clock skew, network issues, power loss, and data corruption can all work to counter the usefulness of real-world time. This is a big problem in modern distributed systems. What use is time though? Time is useful because it lets us tell each other which events happen before other events. This kind of reasoning can be handled in a principled way by making each event mark an explicit predecessor. This is called a vector clock.

If nodes Alice, Bob, and Ann have seen a message (#1) that Bob has $5, Alice has $0, and Ann has $0. Bob wants to take advantage of the really unreliable internet connection between Alice and Ann. He buys a $5 item from Alice (message #2.1) and then quickly buys a $5 from Ann (message #2.2) before Alice and Ann can talk. His goal is for each to see a $5 withdrawal from his account while it has $5, so he ends up with $0. This is a classic example of a race condition.

Bob has seen the double-spend, but he is alright with breaking the protocol. He likely tells everybody else that he only made one of the transactions. At some point, Alice and Ann will synchronize by getting copies of each other's messages. Alice and Ann can both see that there are two messages (2.2 and 2.1) with the same parent message (message #1), and that these two messages alter the values associated with the same key (Bob's account address).

Depending on the protocol, the nodes might decide to accept only the transaction with the smallest numerical hash, might drop both transactions, or might decide to put Bob in debt. By creating an explicit ordering between the events that each node sees, and by building conflict resolution into the protocol, we can ensure that steps taken out of order will eventually converge to the same global state.

It's worth noting that for a moment in time, Bob has gotten away with his crime. This is possible because Alice and Bob's transaction is "done" before Ann comes in. If one desires a system that makes double spending entirely impossible, one could require that all nodes synchronize. This offers its own problems, making it possible for one slow node to halt traffic across the entire system. There is no perfect solution to conflict because each protocol is different. Intelligently balancing scalability with correctness is frequently in the realm of heuristics.

CRYPTOGRAPHIC VERIFICATION

The systems that we will study use cryptography to ensure their invariants. In most cryptographic algorithms, it is much less computationally costly to do things the "right" way than the "wrong" way. Doing things the wrong way involves guessing. Architecting a low probability of accidentally accepting bad data makes this guessing take a very long time. Practical cryptography comes in three disciplines nowadays: symmetric cryptography, asymmetric cryptography, and cryptographic hashing.

Symmetric cryptography is what probably comes to mind when one thinks of "encryption." Somebody has a key and uses it to turn plaintext into ciphertext. This key is then used to get the plaintext from the ciphertext. All of the secrecy lies in this key. This forms a problem when there's no trusted communication medium with the other party to send the key. In a distributed cluster, this is usually the case. Symmetric encryption is fast though, and is safe when the keys never need to be distributed.

Asymmetric cryptography came about as a solution to the key distribution problem. A "handshake" can yield a key for both parties that has never been sent over the wire. Alternatively, we have key pairs composed of the public key and the private key. When one of them encrypts the information, the other one can decrypt it. By publishing the public key everywhere and holding onto the private key, a system for both encryption and signature exists. The private key can "sign" a message that the public key can be used to validate. This proves that the message came from the node it says it came from. The public key can be used to "encrypt" a message that the private key is then used to read. You can combine the two to verify the secret message. This signature is useful because it prevents someone from changing their mind; it is a receipt of the action. Asymmetric encryption is much slower usually. Therefore it is typically used only at first, in order to exchange keys for symmetric encryption. A new symmetric key for each session can thus be used.

Hashing is the last, and potentially the most important cryptographic tool for distributed systems. A hash is a function that takes a huge input domain and squashes it down into a much smaller output domain. These smaller values vary significantly as the input varies just a bit. A cryptographic hash function is made to be moderately fast to run forwards but incredibly slow to find the inverse for a given hash. If one knows that there is a signed hash on a packet, one can say two things about the data in the packet. Either the first sender computed hash one sees from the data one sees, or somebody spent a very long time to find other data with the same hash. This is called a hash collision. If there are verifiable semantics for the data then it's worth noting that the chance of finding a hash collision that looks like it "makes sense" is astronomically low. Typically the data will look pseudorandom.

It should be worth noting that sometimes we do want to blindly guess. Since this requires a brute force attempt that is probabilistically going to be computationally costly, finding any data whose hash has chosen properties is a "proof-of-work." If one has data that hashes to an arbitrarily-chosen hash, then one has evidence that they did the work to find this data. Some systems chain proofs-of-work, so that one has evidence of having done a **lot** of work. As these chains get bigger, it becomes harder and harder for a minority of the cluster to find a longer chain of collisions than the majority of the cluster has computed.

MERKLE EVERYTHING

Large scale distributed systems are all about maintaining the structure of the state held by the cluster. What messages are in flight? What references in which data structures should point where? What order should things be in the queue? There are a lot of things to track. Should we expect every node to hold onto all of it? Is the cluster always right, or does it eventually stabilize? Can we tell when it has? It's tempting to say that the invariants of the data structure, a global property, should be handled by "those trusted people" but there are usually no trusted peers in a distributed system. In order to provide a reliable service, we need to design the way that untrusted nodes manipulate data so that if the crypto checks out we know that we can trust the data as much as we trust the node which signed it.

The answer to this is the idea of the hash-associated-pointer. Data structures in the box-and-pointer model are constructed from allocation "blocks" which contain both pieces of data and references to other blocks. These blocks can be memory addresses, IP addresses, or keys into an associative structure. We can associated a hash of the pointed-to data with the reference. This is referred to as a Merkle tree when done with a tree, but there are "Merkle" versions of any data structure. It's worth noting that because the hash and the pointer must be updated together, updates must be atomic.

The idea behind a Merkle tree is that it is a set of compressed "proofs" that pieces of data are trusted. If I want to check if a piece of data is located in a tree which is an order of magnitude larger than my local storage, I must ask the cluster of untrusted peers. Any peer might respond, and might give me data that the cluster didn't agree to incorporate. Merkle trees allow me to check that the data is indeed in the cluster's collection of trusted state.

Consider a hypothetical Merkle tree. After joining the cluster, I fetch a hash of the root of the tree from a source that's been signed with the key of one or more trusted peers. If enough untrusted peers sign it, we typically trust the cluster at large and so trust it. I can then ask the cluster for the interior of the tree. It's worth noting that I don't need the entire tree. In this way, I need only get the single hash at the top of the tree from a trusted source. Any untrusted peer can give me the rest of the data structure.

A more rudimentary example of hash-associated-pointers is the use of Distributed Hash Tables, where data is replicated throughout the cluster and the hash is used to search for the data and to find the peer responsible for the data. Trust is placed in the assertion that if the fetched data has the hash that the data was submitted to the network with, then the fetched data is most likely the same data that was first submitted.

MERKLE STRUCTURES AS PROOFS OF HISTORY

An interesting interpretation of Merkle structures are as proofs of constructability. Let's imagine that I have a system which says that any peer can report another peer trying to fill the system with duplicate requests. In this case, peers are told to drop traffic from this attacking peer. How do we prevent attacking peers from reporting innocent peers, while preventing peers from being overwhelmed by checking these reports?

If a peer has inserted service requests into the global state, then they should exist in the Merkle structure which organizes this state. We assume that peers sign their service requests. We would make an interval tree which tracks times of requests. By providing the paths to the attacker's requests, a good peer can verify that the maximum number of requests have been inserted into the tree in this interval. After checking that we've put these requests in the interval tree, we can insert this attacker into the associative Merkle tree which uses peer hashes as keys. This requires a number of tree accesses which is logarithmic in the number of service requests and in the number of blacklisted peers.

In the future, new peers which forward this attacker's message can be told that this attacker is banned. Good peers will send the path to the hash of the attacker in the blacklist, and other peers can verify that they're in the blacklist. In this way, we have added rate limiting to the global cluster without requiring that any one peer has more power than the others. If any peer misbehaves, all good peers will stop communicating with them.

Chapter 2

HOW TOR WORKS

Intro to Onion Routing and Partial Observability

INTRO

The Tor network is a public distributed network which uses cryptography to provide probabilistic anonymity. It establishes TCP streams from one end of a global cluster of untrusted proxies to the other, hiding traffic source information while allowing bidirectional network traffic over the stream. We will study how intelligent network architecture as well as cryptography allows for this real life system to provide service in the face of coordinated attacks by very powerful adversaries.

THREAT MODEL AND GOALS

Tor differs from many principled distributed architectures in that the primary concern is usability. Rather than making promises about the security of the system and accepting usability restrictions, Tor promises that it can be used for Web traffic and interactive applications. As we will see later, this informs the decision to accept a certain level of vulnerability to timing attacks.

At first, Tor's goal was to allow for privacy of traffic. It should be unfeasible for an eavesdropper or hostile network member to uniquely identify the source of a given TCP packet that leaves the network. As many people who require privacy live in countries where the network is blocked, state-level attackers comprise many of Tor's series adversaries. This expanded Tor's threat model to include resistance to censorship from an adversary capable of enumerating many machines and completely controlling traffic within an IP range. This has motivated changes in relay discovery since the initial Tor architecture.

ONION ROUTING 101

Imagine that one wanted to get a packet from Alice's computer to Bob's web server. Let's say that Alice lives in a country where people who shop for pressure cookers and backpacks get raids from federal agents. Now Bob sells a lot of household items and he unfortunately his ISP has been compelled by the government to give them all of his traffic. Alice doesn't want to get raided because her neighbors are light sleepers. How can we get Alice's packet to Bob without giving the government somebody to intimidate, pay, or torture to get the information?

So the first idea is for Alice to have a friend carry the packets along for her. She sets up a TLS connection with a web proxy on her friend's server. This friend lets anybody on the internet use it, so the government has no idea which of the 10k citizens are shopping for things on the naughty list. This has some terrible properties though.

This server is now "trusted." This isn't "trusted" in the sense that it's trustworthy, but "trusted" in that you must trust this relay with the entirety of your security. If this server is run in Alice's country, or her country is an ally of the country the server runs in, her friend running the server might get raided. Friends don't get friends raided. Also, the issue of timing and packet size comes into play. If an attacker watches all of the traffic coming in and out of the proxy, and if Alice is the only one sending a packet every 50ms with a 2kb payload, then the attacker can trivially associate Alice's input with the proxy's output.

What if you were to chain together multiple proxies? You have the same problems without cryptography. Every proxy is potentially the weakest link in the chain. You have a weaker, not a stronger system. Now let's give every proxy a public/private key pair. You could encrypt the message for the last proxy, and now all of the other proxies can't read it. Furthermore, the last proxy only knows the address of the server sending the message to it. If the attacker shows up at their door, they can explain that they're unable to help without lying. The issue now is that all of the proxies before the last in the chain know the address of the last proxy. This means that the first proxy in the chain sees both Alice's IP address and the IP address of the last proxy; the first proxy can tell the attacker everything it needs to know.

What you do is that you encrypt the message with the public key for the last proxy first. Then you create a message for the next-to-last server saying "send this encrypted message to the proxy with this IP". You encrypt this message with the public key for the next to last proxy. You do this for each step in the chain until you reach the first proxy. You can encrypt with the public key for this relay, but Tor doesn't because Tor connects Alice to the first proxy with TLS. TLS is already secured using public key cryptography.

In Chapter 1, we discussed how public key cryptography is much slower than symmetric cryptography. If you were to use it for all of the packets as we described, you'd have a very slow network. Also, a government would be able to go to each proxy server owner and make them decrypt the given packet because the proxy's public/private key pair remains the same. Instead, we can use public key cryptography to agree on a symmetric encryption key for each server. Now we still encrypt the packet in layers from last relay to first relay, but we use a temporary key that is fast to use. At the end of every hour or so, all of these proxies must throw away their keys. It's typically outside of an attacker's power to seize many servers spanning many countries within an hour. This is called perfect forward secrecy because a security breach in the future doesn't jeopardize the security of past traffic.

This doesn't prevent the timing attack which we spoke about. The Tor network could work around this problem by collecting all of the messages to send in each 10-minute period, add padding on the end of each message to get a uniform size, and shuffle them all around. The Tor project chose not to do this because it would make the system unsuitable for interactive web browsing. Instead, the Tor network has decided that this is a failure state. The Tor project has a number of strategies to make it unlikely for a single attacker to be able to observe enough of the exit relays and enough of the entry relays into the network to correlate messages via size and timing. These don't always work. Later we will cover the most recent and most successful attack on the Tor network.

CIRCUITS AND CONNECTION POOLING

If you need to service many requests, it's very important to balance the network load across many machines. When a client needs to use Tor, they will create a route through the network with an entry point and an exit point. This is called a circuit.

Onion routing as it had existed before Tor would simply create a new circuit for each TCP connection that the user needed. The issue with this is that some web traffic patterns can create and dispose of hundreds of connections regularly. In order to achieve the promise of usability, Tor has an interesting connection pooling architecture that tries to reuse routes through the network (called circuits).

When a client tries to connect to the network, they will first get a list of the relays they can use. From this, they will choose an exit relay, a guard (entry) relay, and one intermediate relay. Tor will make sure that these relays are geographically far apart, and are not hosted by the same people (self-reported). We will later explain the differences in relay types. We only choose 3 hops because adding more hops doesn't really add security. Each relay can only know the predecessor and successor, so 3 hops will provide the required amount of isolation. Furthermore circuits with more hops must go through more servers, increasing the likelihood that an attacker's server is included in this chain.

Once a client has chosen the relays to use, it will connect to the guard relay over TLS. Since TLS uses secure, fast communication with good key negotiation, there is no other crypto used between the client and the guard server. The client will then send "Cells" (tor protocol packets) which tell the guard relay to connect to the intermediate relay. Cells can be commands for relays, or can be data payload packets. Further cells are sent to the intermediate relay in order to carry out a Diffie-Hellman key negotiation. After this is done, the intermediate relay is likewise commanded to extend the circuit to the exit relay.

It's worth noting that it is important to use integrity checking on these data streams. While an attacker can't read the messages, if an attacker could guess the plaintext then they could find out the stream of bits that were used to encrypt this specific packet. Future packets are not compromised by this, but the attacker gains the ability to modify the message. Certain steps in the protocol can be modified, and the network can have protocol invariants broken.

TCP packets which are sent through Tor after this circuit is built will move through these connections, encrypted symmetrically for each relay. At the exit relay, the final plaintext message is visible. Since circuits are shared for different TCP connections, it is the duty of the exit relay to make sure that the packet is put into the correct TCP stream. This works in most cases, but puts the burden of traffic cleanliness on the user. A classic example was the issue of BitTorrent.

BitTorrent will embed the IP address of the user in the data packets. This means that anybody seeing a BitTorrent packet leave the Tor network can associate it with the client on the other end. Even worse, an attacker can associate this exit relay with the circuit which is tunneling all of the client's TCP streams. Because of attacks like this, Tor now will use a new circuit for certain kinds of traffic such as building a circuit, sending a message, hosting a hidden service, or joining as a relay or exit relay. BitTorrent is still bad to run over Tor, but most Tor clients can try to prevent it from sharing circuits with Web traffic.

DIRECTORY SYSTEM

Alice has a messy problem in the above system. If she doesn't know any of the proxy operators, how does she find a collection of trustworthy proxies to route in this onion method? If the relays that she chooses is from a small enough collection, then the risk of identification increases. How does she prevent an attacker from sending her a list of relays which only include bad relays?

This is where Tor's directory system comes into play. The directory system is a collection of router descriptors and states. The directory system of Tor is actually not distributed. It's decentralized to a degree. There are currently eight directory authorities for the deployed Tor cluster, but it managed to operate with only three for the longest time. These authorities have their public keys and hard-coded into the software distribution of Tor. That reliance upon this system of a handful servers has remained cryptographically protected against nation-states for so long is quite a surprise.

This system has gone through three changes. At first, these servers were fully trusted. Clients would connect to all three servers and would get the state of the cluster from the most recent one spoken to. They got this document directly and it was sent without encryption. When authorities disagreed, clients would get different documents. Even worse, an attacker could tell which document each client got. They knew which relays clients could use. Also, there was no consensus between all three servers that was required. Lastly, each server was subject to the load of the entire cluster. This fundamentally threatened the ability of Tor to scale.

1.   The first major change was to separate the data into a document of relay attributes and a document of relay states. The latter could be used to keep a consistent view of the subset of the cluster that is available both during the state fetch and the last descriptor fetch. This state document was much cheaper to send.

2.   The second change was to prevent rogue authorities from controlling a client's view of the network. This was done by fetching a more complex

document from each authority which represented their view of the network. This allowed clients to find the intersection of trust between the authorities, potentially partitioning clients based on document variation throughout time. Since the documents were sent unencrypted, fingerprinting was feasible. Attacks in this vein could allow an attacker to eventually narrow down traffic sources. This moved more load from the authorities to the clients. Connecting to the network now required fetching a few megabytes of descriptors.

3. The last major change was to explicitly create a consensus document. The authorities will find a consensus view of the network once per hour using an ad-hoc consensus algorithm. They will all sign this view of the network and will distribute it for the next hour. This document used a much compressed format of router descriptors, saving space. This gives all clients a consistent view of the network and decreases the footprint of the directory documents. Clients will now sometimes create a one-hop Tor connection to fetch the next document. This prevents an attacker from fingerprinting documents and profiling which clients see which network states propagate.

HOW DOES A RELAY JOIN THE TOR CLUSTER?

What's interesting about the Tor cluster is that bandwidth allocation is integrated into it. A non-exit relay starts trying to join the cluster by forming four circuits to itself and sending a benchmark self-test to measure the bandwidth it can carry. This it put into a router descriptor and signed and is offered to the directory authorities. Here we see that the directory authorities are acting as public key distribution agents much like CA authorities do in the HTTP world.

At first, the cluster doesn't trust you. It won't really route much traffic (if any) through you. This routing is done by reporting your bandwidth availability in the consensus document. Clients will choose you with a probability proportional to your bandwidth availability, and so few clients will choose you for a circuit. All the while though, relays in the network will measure you. If they find you fast and stable, they'll slowly allocate more and more traffic to you. As your traffic slice increases, your circuit speeds will be measured to find out what you can really provide.

You'll get more traffic but it will be limited still because you won't be a guard relay. If every circuit is new then the chance of not picking an attacker's relays for the first and last hops goes to 0 over enough time.

If you remain with the first hop over time, then you either choose an attacker and lose any time your other relays are attacker relays or you choose a good relay and all of your paths are safe. This stable first relay must be reliable or the performance will be terrible. This relay is a guard relay. This is essentially a way to make it more probable to be safe.

For you to become a guard relay you must be stable for 8 days. After you're a guard relay you'll be moved up into a separate class of relay which is rotated through by clients over time. Eventually the number of clients that cycle out of you will equal the number which cycle in. You will have your bandwidth mostly saturated at this point.

If you were an exit relay, you would see traffic leaving you with speed once your bandwidth allocation was being scaled up.

CONCLUSION

We see here that the use of cryptography as well as the properties of network bandwidth and geographic IP allocation allows the Tor network to put up a strong defense against adversaries with nation-state resources. It's interesting to see here the architectural assumptions that allowing some relays to be evil requires. One must protect against data traffic injection, misuse of the protocol, observation of traffic, malicious saturation of the network, and malicious dishonesty about traffic statistics. And it's through the miracle of public key cryptography that we can negotiate data transmission contracts with potentially hostile relays.

I find the heterogeneous nature of Tor quite interesting. There is the decentralized cluster state authority system which uses a small number of trusted people to verify the truth of network observations. The actual routing policy partitions relays into where they will be on the paths through the relays. In each and every step, a relay is only allowed to perform the steps that we expect it to achieve from past behavior. Throughout all of this, we see that a fungible resource is used to make attacking Tor from the inside expensive. This resource is bandwidth over time; this resource is identity.

Attackers tend to use anonymity to make attacks cheap to carry out. A computer can participate in a denial of service attack or inject traffic frequently by changing IP address. We do not put a relay in a position to degrade the network until it has behaved well for a long time. After placing it there, we constantly observe it. When it behaves badly, we eject it from the network. We see that the cost of attacking Tor is the maintenance and loss of a cryptographically-verified trustworthy identity which must be maintained at the cost of network bandwidth. By assuming that every network member is anonymous, the Tor protocol intelligently creates an economy of trust and makes untrustworthiness expensive.

RESOURCES

http://css.csail.mit.edu/6.858/2014/readings/tor-design.pdf

https://www.youtube.com/watch?v=rIf_VZQr-dw

https://blog.torproject.org/blog/top-changes-tor-2004-design-paper-part-1

https://blog.torproject.org/blog/top-changes-tor-2004-design-paper-part-2

https://blog.torproject.org/blog/top-changes-tor-2004-design-paper-part-3

https://blog.torproject.org/blog/lifecycle-of-a-new-relay

https://www.torproject.org/docs/hidden-services.html.en

http://arstechnica.co.uk/security/2016/08/building-a-new-tor-that-withstands-next-generation-state-surveillance/

Chapter 3

HOW I2P WORKS

Distributing Peer Trust

INTRO

I2P is an onion routing network very similar to Tor which seeks to address architectural decisions that many think make Tor an easier target for a powerful attacker. I2P doesn't use a centralized handful of Directory Servers, instead using distributed hash tables (DHTs hereafter) to coordinate state. The design of I2P is heavily distributed and router roles are much more homogenous than Tor. This is enabled by not allowing connections out of the network. All services in I2P are what Tor would call hidden services. Many would say that design makes it harder for an adversary to observe I2P participants and coerce them into leaving. Others would say that I2P's smaller size makes it easier for attackers to flood with evil peers. We will consider the utility of I2P's response to its threat model.

THREAT MODEL

I2P's network is small, much smaller than Tor. Despite designing to scale to millions of users, it suffers from the privacy issues of small anonymity networks. Many attacks which should be impossible are tractable to a state-level attacker.

If I2P is deemed to be illegal in a country, a sufficiently motivated attacker may make efforts to identify I2P users and summarily jail them. As all routers are stored globally in the DHT, this is a more realistic attack than one would think. The built-in rate limiting in the DHT system makes this less effective, but it is an attack nonetheless.

It's not that easy to simply observe I2P traffic and to know that it's I2P traffic. Every byte is encrypted or part of the handshake, making it harder to isolate from other encrypted TCP. The use of randomized ports across TCP and UDP also makes it harder to fingerprint.

An active adversary with passive widespread surveillance is an entirely different matter though. An ISP colluding with an agent connected to the network could have the agent send a peer data of certain sizes. Over time, peers sending less data can be ruled out until only the recipient is left. This attack is practical in a small network like I2P. Similarly, timing attacks can apply. They're much harder in I2P though, due to queuing, message batching, and throttling. This kind of attacker is rare, as attacks can be quite costly since they tend to require global attacks in order to isolate single peers.

More reasonable is for an attacker to take on the entire network by creating many evil nodes. Eventually, a good portion of the network will route through only the attacker's nodes. As the network grows, this becomes more difficult. This is known as a Sybil attack. There are token protections against this type of attack. For instance, peers from the same IP range won't be in the same tunnel. This is not even remotely sufficient though. If an attacker controls 20% of the peers in the network, they can refuse to route messages unless predecessors and successors are both bad nodes. This will force a tunnel with only the attacker's nodes, or will prevent the peer from using I2P at all.

This brings up a good point. An attacker doesn't need to break into I2P if they can make it unusable to their target group. By applying load to the network, I2P's latency can be increased until clients will be forced to abandon it. This is an effective attack. I2P has safeguards and throttling at many layers, but a motivated adversary could still degrade the system with enough evil peers.

Lastly, the distributed nature of I2P's DHTs make them a target for attack. The fact that a router advertising a public key will sign their information with it makes it very difficult to insert information which has much of an effect. The DHT-serving routers have rate limiting, and there are many of them. This makes a denial of service attack much harder, since peers can route around nodes under stress. Stressing the entire DHT system is expensive, but doable. The current mitigations are considered imperfect but competitive.

TUNNEL CREATION

The routing differences between Tor and I2P stem primarily from the fact that I2P doesn't connect to the public internet by default. Tunnels in I2P work slightly similarly to how hidden services work in Tor, but are faster because I2P was designed with hidden services as the primary use. It comes down in part to the fact that a Tor Hidden Service requires more initial connection coordination and requires more intermediate relays to send the message along.

Tunnels are much shorter-lived in I2P by design than in Tor. Whereas Tor will multiplex messages through a long-lived circuit, I2P's tunnel policy makes this tunnel conservation less useful. Tunnels in I2P are unidirectional; every client has a different set of routers for outgoing traffic than they do for incoming traffic. This partitions the nodes along the tunnel into roles which each behave differently. This is quite similar to Tor's Guard/Intermediate/Exit relay system works, with some important differences.

In the tunnel pipeline, the "Gateway", "Participant" and "Endpoint" router roles correspond to the Guard, Intermediate, and Exit relay roles respectively. There are zero-hop, one-hop, two-hop, and three-hop tunnels. Tor's standard architecture is to use three-hop tunnels, and I2P recommends three-hop tunnels for maximum effective security. We explained why this policy makes sense in the previous chapter.

Alice ->

Outbound Gateway ->

Outbound Participant -> Outbound Endpoint -
>

Inbound Gateway ->

Inbound Participant -> Inbound Endpoint ->

Bob

The Gateway is responsible for receiving a number of messages and batching them up into a datum called a "garlic message." Garlic messages will be encrypted by the Gateway and passed along to the first Participant. The Participants know very little, and simply removes a layer of encryption to read the forwarding address and passes the message along to the next Participant or the Endpoint. The Endpoint must decrypt the garlic message and figure out what to do with it. We see above that Alice's Endpoint talks to Bob's Gateway. The role of Gateway/Participant/Endpoint in the pipeline is fixed, Alice's Endpoint doesn't talk to Bob's Endpoint.

Note that Alice doesn't necessarily need to choose the same Outbound Gateway every time. I2P has not chosen to use Guard nodes as Tor has. This makes it more likely for an attacker which can run a Sybil attack to force a peer to rapidly recreate tunnels and eventually route through only attacker nodes. On the other hand, Tor's Guard nodes have a recent history of poisoning [https://blog.torproject.org/blog/tor-security-advisory-relay-early-traffic-confirmation-attack]. The fact that you're choosing from a smaller pool of relays for Guards can make it easier for a patient attacker to control a fraction of the Guards.

Also note that there is no single computer which appears to be the source of all of the traffic. In Tor, the Exit Node will appear to the outside world to be the source of all traffic it routes outbound. This requires heroic volunteers willing to defend themselves from government agencies who observe illegal traffic. Rather than getting a large pool of people who hope that "I'm running Tor" is enough to avoid culpability for exit node traffic, I2P makes it so that only Bob can see the traffic destined for Bob. On the other hand, Bob must be running an I2P service for this to work. By requiring that all participants hosting services do so through I2P, the legal risk associated with relays of the network are decreased.

This latter point is why I2P tends to have higher peer participation than Tor. Tor has relays and Tor has clients, and only a few committed souls are both. Most I2P clients with reliable internet connections become routers for other peers. By making it less costly to route traffic, I2P ensures that the routing capabilities will scale with the network. Contrast this to the problems that the Tor network would face if the relay set remained the same but the number of clients were to increase tenfold. The directory service and the onion routing of Tor would face traffic saturation. This also makes it harder for an adversary to ban all I2P routers. Tor's relays are more fixed than I2P's, requiring more obfuscation and centralized secret accumulation (bridge relay list) to avoid state-level attackers from banning them.

ONION ROUTING TRANSIT CRYPTOGRAPHY

Unlike circuits in the Tor network, I2P tunnels are much shorter lived. Furthermore the use of separate tunnels for incoming and outgoing traffic makes it difficult for a peer to associate a key with a specific message. This makes the Tor policy of negotiating an AES shared key with each relay in the circuit slightly too simplistic for I2P. Instead, I2P uses an interesting system of explicitly-managed key reuse.

When an I2P router wants to coordinate communication with a router, the sending router will use the asymmetric cryptosystem ElGamal (a Diffie-Hellman variant) to encrypt an AES256 key (called the SessionKey) for use in future communication streams. Rather than stopping here, the sending router will also create a number of SessionTags and encrypt them in the message body. Each SessionTag is a 32-bit random nonce, which is an arbitrary number that can be associated with at most one message. When the receiving router gets this message, it will store the AES256 key in a key/value system with the SessionTags as keys. Since SessionTags can only be used once, routers must re-negotiate a new SessionKey after all SessionTags are used up.

When future messages are received, the router will check if the first 32 bytes are a SessionTag. If so, then the router will use the SessionKey associated with that SessionTag to decrypt the message. This removes the SessionTag from the router's collection. This makes it impossible for an adversary to notice a reused SessionTag, and infer that the same two routers are responsible for these messages. If the first 32 bytes are not, then the router tries to decrypt the message using asymmetric encryption. If the decrypted payload has a correct checksum then the SessionTags and SessionKey are taken from the message body. Otherwise, it is refused.

In order for the sending router to know that the SessionTag handshake completed correctly, it will frequently bundle information for the inbound tunnel into the message. The router can then send back an acknowledgement of correct communication. It's worth repeating one more time that I2P tunnels are unidirectional, unlike Tor, so these SessionKeys are used for communication in only one direction. This limits the ability for an adversary to compromise communication in one direction and get the entire message stream.

THE DISTRIBUTED NETWORK DATABASE

Rather than rely on a centralized set of directory servers, like Tor, I2P uses two distributed hash tables to coordinate the state of the network. This offers added scalability. There are 10 Tor directory servers at the time of writing. (Find them at https://atlas.torproject.org/#search/flag:authority) These are trusted servers; the integrity of the entire Tor consensus rests on them being good actors. In contrast, I2P puts the data in the hands of everybody and the trust in the hands of nobody.

As we will later get to, all routers in I2P have their traffic rates measured in a trustworthy way. It's not entirely self-reported. This means that we have a reliable way to figure out which peers are the fastest and most accessible to a given router. These routers are called "floodfill" routers and are used to carry the Network Database.

In a recurring theme in these systems, we gain resilience against compromise through public key cryptography. A router publishes a public key and a list of attributes associated with the itself, and signs the message cryptographically. When a router wants to insert data into NetDB, it picks a floodfill router and sends it the data. It waits 10 seconds and then picks another floodfill router and requests the information. If it can't find the information, then it repeats this. Eventually, the network accepts the insert.

Insertion works by doing an XOR with the hash of the key and each floodfill router hash to find the value of the distance. The closest floodfill routers will get the value pushed to them. This redundancy builds peer loss tolerance into the DHT. Because there is a redundancy of 8x currently, and because the network is small currently, we have a O(1) rather than a O(log n) query.

I2P has two DHTs required to build tunnels. There are the RouterInfo and the LeaseSet, both of which use the SHA256 of a router's "identity" public key as the key. The RouterInfo table describes the attributes of the peer's I2P router which is connected to the network. The router's identity public key, IP address, capabilities, and a hash of the above are inserted into the network. LeaseSets describe the inbound router to use as the starting point (Gateway router below) for the tunnel. It also describes a key to use when talking to that router to uniquely identify the particular tunnel that is used for inbound connections. RouterInfos do not expire by default, peers will manage a local cache as per client preferences. LeaseSets do expire because inbound tunnels expire.

PEER PROFILING

If a peer could lie about their performance in the RouterInfo, then an adversary could force the network to route a lot of traffic through a few slow nodes. This would make the network unusable, a very effective attack. RouterInfo only allows peers to say "I'm too slow to be useful." I2P, like Tor, will measure the performance of peers so as to accurately route traffic between them. Over time, the capacity and speed will be found.

This allows peers to be sorted into three groups: high capacity, fast, and standard. High capacity routers have a capacity higher than their peers. A fast router is a high capacity router which is faster than the median speed of the router's peers. Standard routers are the remaining routers.

Peers snoop on each other and create profiles on their tunnel drop rate, their NetDB response latency, and other attributes. A router saves their peers' profiles to disk on shutdown, to make rejoining the network easier. Clients are expected to determine eviction rate of profiles.

PEER SELECTION

Peers are selected from the "fast" group when the router is going to be used to communicate with a hosted service on another peer. Peers are selected from the standard group randomly for tasks that are acceptable to have low bandwidth, such as DHT lookups and client tunnel test packets. These "exploratory" tunnels will fall back on fast routers when the standard routers begin to provide too much latency.

The I2P architecture dictates certain important restrictions on the peers that can be chosen when creating a tunnel in the name of security. The following are forbidden:

• Two peers from the same /16 IP space may not be in the same tunnel.

• A peer may participate in a maximum of 33% of all tunnels created by the router.

• Peers with extremely low bandwidth are not used.

• Peers for which a recent connection attempt failed are not used.

It's also worth noting that an ordering is applied to all peers in order to avoid the Predecessor attack [http://forensics.umass.edu/pubs/wright-tissec.pdf] . That is, if node A comes before node B in a tunnel then node A will always come before B in all tunnels.

CONCLUSIONS

We've looked at a second variation on the classic design of onion routing. I2P is an interesting architecture because of the aggressively decentralized nature of it. Going after I2P peers offers little benefit, as routers are fairly homogenous. Likewise the lack of a connection to the public internet means that no exit node is required. There is no peer both listening to and transmitting the plaintext of this outbound traffic for sites to point a finger at. This more insular network containing only hidden services looks like a solution which can scale indefinitely as nodes are added. Some of the algorithms related to peer manipulation and search may need to be improved at some point, but these changes would not require major protocol revision. If the world changed in such a way that secure communication was more important to most than access to mainstream social networking, I2P looks like a fine network to take on the challenge.

RESOURCES

http://blog.torproject.org/blog/one-cell-enough

http://wwwcip.informatik.uni-erlangen.de/~spjsschl/i2p.pdf

https://geti2p.net/_static/pdf/I2P-PET-CON-2009.1.pdf

https://geti2p.net

http://forensics.umass.edu/pubs/wright-tissec.pdf

Chapter 4

HOW BITCOIN WORKS

on the Power of Immutable History

INTRO

Imagine a lawless land where only other lands' money was trusted. Doing business with them was slow, often hazardous. Theft was possible, because you paid people by giving them a copy of the key (credit card information) to your personal gold vault. This was unsafe, but you didn't know how to do commerce any other way. The point of sale needed to be instant, and the sale was often so far from home.

Now imagine, a new casino appeared which was larger than most amusement parks and wanted a stable internal currency for the significant transactions. In this lawless land, they didn't want to have people walking around with currency that could be stolen. They wanted something like gold, but they didn't want gold. They gave people checkbooks and promised them there was gold somewhere behind the money. As long as people believed in the added value, it existed. The economy grew and it became more valued for its use as a currency.

Eventually, the casino was made non-profit. It had a controlled rate of releasing this new currency and started letting anybody work for it at any time of the day, paying them this currency.

The bank worked in an odd way. The volunteers watched customers' messages come up and ask for transactions to be made. They'd collect a certain quantity of them and go to check that they all followed the rules. They follow a specific policy for how to throw out transactions that can't happen at the same time. These transactions are signed with the customer's secrets, so they are definitely from the listed customers. After they check it, they store the correct transactions in-order in a signed envelope (Merkle tree) . They pay themselves a little bit at the start of each envelope, but customers also pay a little extra in the transaction for the worker. The worker must now go to the strangest machine in the land.

The bank distributed a machine which examines the signed envelope and spits out a custom lottery game. This game was very slow, and the poor volunteer has to go through the process of playing the lottery until he wins.

But it gets worse.

If another lottery player collected a copy of that same quantity of messages, they could also start playing the lottery. And they're almost certainly going to be. They might start before or after, but it doesn't really matter. A million losses doesn't make *the next lottery ticket any more likely to be a winner. Each event is independent.*

If they win first, then their envelope goes into the casino's history ledger and they get the reward they paid themselves. All of your lottery playing is for nothing.

We should clarify that lottery playing doesn't make anybody money when a loss occurs. This lottery is entirely done for the people and by the people.

Eventually, people decided to team up and share the rewards. Big clubs of lottery players formed which promised a payout equivalent to the work done. People were happy, and they played on. After a day's pay, they took their coin home and spread it far throughout the economy.

Ordering of events in a distributed system is a hard problem. It's one of the hard problems in Computer Science. Even if all of the packets are sent in the same order to all peers, having multiple sources of events means that events are doomed to be reordered. Some of the time, this doesn't matter. Most of the internet is optimized around the idea of allowing unrelated transactions to be reordered and buffered. Unfortunately, sometimes it is necessary to have the entire network agree on a linear history.

This is the case in systems where exposed actions can make resources inaccessible. An example is currency; a person is only able to spend funds for the small window in time that they own them. Blockchain technologies form an explicit linear ordering of synchronized operations enforced in a distributed manner.

The name comes from the fact that the envelopes from the story above are called "blocks" in Bitcoin. Transactions fill blocks, which have lotteries played over them through proof-of-work. This process is called "mining". The democratic mob votes on a history of transactions to accept by gambling at hash values.

While the first lottery writer might have won a reward from the casino in our parable, the reward only holds if it holds in the longest chain of history. Good nodes will reject the invalid transaction history in the mined transaction chunk (block), and will collectively play the odds better than the bad actor. They will eventually catch up. The good history will grow larger, and the bad actor will lose it all.

ECONOMICS

The value of Bitcoin is set by supply and demand, like everything else in economics. Relative prices for goods between currencies should be stable, else people label it arbitrage and abuse it until it is fixed. This means that the value of Bitcoin is a consensus had by people on how much utility there is in being able to spend Bitcoins.

If people are willing to exchange fifty metal coins for a Bitcoin, then a Bitcoin is worth your currency's equivalent of fifty metal coins. If Bitcoins are more difficult to find in your corner of the world, then they might be worth more. If Bitcoins can buy more, then they're worth more. If Bitcoins are more convenient, then they're worth more. If Bitcoins are cheaper to use, then they're worth more.

THREAT MODEL

Bitcoin's only tractable attack is an attack on the integrity of the blockchain's linear history. Bitcoin is a set of rules for creating a data structure, the blockchain. The rules assume that whomever owns the private key associated with Bitcoins is the owner of the Bitcoins. When the customer wants to place a transaction, they need to sign the transaction. The ability to sign a transaction is a proof that one has the private key associated with the public key that the Bitcoin was last sent to. The "last sent to" part is the reason that a linear history is necessary.

If you try to spend Bitcoin that has already been spent, the mining nodes will reject your message. The only real practical attack on the blockchain is to spend Bitcoins at a vendor, get the service after the transaction is in the blockchain, and then mine a block that has you sending the Bitcoin elsewhere. This "history rewriting" requires the attacker to do the proof-of-work for all blocks after the rewritten one. Bitcoin specifies that the longest chain is the one that is correct. This means that the attacker needs to outrace the rest of the network in order to convince them to accept the evil fork.

The farther back in history, the more work that an attacker must do to catch up with the rest of the network and overcome them. This means that after a number of blocks have been mined, transactions are more or less unable to be altered. This gives the system a consensus on the linear ordering of transactions. Note though that integrity depends on the majority of the network choosing a chain that can be verified.

CRYPTOGRAPHY USED

Bitcoin uses HashCash for proof-of-work. HashCash works much like the lottery metaphor above. One has a block of information to hash, including a nonce that is the miner's current lottery guess. The work difficulty is set by requiring the worker's nonce make the SHA256 hash lower than a given value. The output hash will vary in an unpredictable way as the nonce is incremented, making this search a pseudorandom Poisson process. Bitcoin has a rather difficult proof-of-work. Every two weeks, the Bitcoin network calibrates the current proof-of-work difficulty to reflect capacities.

The other major use of cryptography in Bitcoin is the use of public key cryptography to handle a person's account balance. The transaction sends the currency to a person's public key. The private key associated with this public key then gains the power of that currency. The funds holder can sign transactions and smart contracts with this key to express consent.

SEQUENCE OF PROOFS

That brings us to a powerful alternate view of the blockchain that is the reason why it generalizes. It's not a key-value store of bank balances. It's a sequence of proofs. The existence of the completed proof-of-work is proof of the existence of the payout coins. Every future transaction with the coins refers to the transaction which created the coins being spent. It is the burden of the network to assert that you are referring to the latest state of that resource.

Consider instead a system of games of chess with betting. Each transaction "pays" the turn to the next payer, with alteration. Checking board rules would fall to the miners. You can prevent turn alteration this way.

Consider instead a blockchain that began with a number of facts and implications, along with implications such as Modus Ponens. From these, you could make each transaction identify itself as a usage of a reasoning rule, and it could refer back to the pieces of data which inhabit it. The proof checking would only have to check the latest transaction, as the assumptions of the proof being fulfilled are asserted to be true because they are older than it in the blockchain. Reasoned, accountable arguments could be carried out this way.

SCALABILITY PROBLEMS

The previous chess network would be miserable to use in all likelihood. If the proof-of-work is sufficiently hard, then it should take minutes to get a move accepted by the blockchain. Interactive applications seeking to use the blockchain run up against many issues. Current Bitcoin mining even runs up against this problem. Long transaction times result from the throughput limitations built into the Bitcoin network by setting the difficulty.

This difficulty pushes miners to turn toward pools. As mining pools control a larger and larger fraction of the world's mining power, the Bitcoin network suddenly becomes dependent on these mining pools being good actors. The distributed system of Bitcoin becomes a decentralized system, compromising many of the initial promises.

This stems from the fact that proof-of-work is inherently costly. There are other ways to address the problems of double spending, which we will cover. Most of the problems related to Bitcoin is due to incorrect usage of Bitcoin. Bitcoin is designed to be a ledger which has the last word. It promises linear, strong consistency between transactions on the blockchain. Many applications are alright with eventual consistency. We will see that it is possible to conduct business off of the blockchain which can then have the state at the end of the session persist.

SOLUTIONS

Proof of Stake And Tattling

A potential solution to the growing pains of Bitcoin is the use of proof-of-stake rather than proof-of-work. An attacker which has a stake in the history already on the blockchain is unlikely to jeopardize it. In proof-of-stake, the cryptocurrency is paid by the miners into the bets of the next block to win. If an attacker bets on multiple chains, then they're guaranteed to lose money. This, combined with the fact that buying a lot of currency is more expensive than a lot of computer power, makes proof-of-stake practical. We will cover Peercoin later, which does proof of stake and has other mitigations for certain attacks.

An interesting idea is vote tattling. When an attacker votes on one block with a predecessor, and then votes on another with the same predecessor, peers can observe this. They can report double voting by using the votes as cryptographically-verified evidence, and taking the attacker's vote-money.

Micro-Payments

Many times, entities want low-latency transactions over a short duration of time. Betting, bars, and moonlighting with frequent and small rewards are all examples. In order to achieve that, micropayment channels can be used.

Bitcoin has the ability to represent fairly complex transactions, much more complex than simple money exchange. The transactions are written around a number of simple opcodes. One such opcode gives ability to hold locked funds until a certain timeframe has elapsed.

Note also, that Bitcoin transactions have their own meanings even before being entered in the blockchain. These two facts allow people to set up a channel of payments. In a payment channel, the sender places a certain amount of money under time-lock. Until the time specified in the Bitcoin transaction, the sender can't access their funds unless the receiver allows them to. Now the receiver can have the sender sign Bitcoin transactions of increasingly larger value as the payments accumulate down the channel.

None of these signed transactions are published until the channel is closed. When closed, the receiver publishes the latest signed transaction. It ends the time-lock and sends the confirmed funds to the receiver and refunds the remaining funds to the sender. If the receiver doesn't finish this handshake, and sacrifices their payments, then the transaction times out and the sender can do whatever they like with the locked funds.

Monero

One issue that should be jumping out to the attentive reader is that Bitcoin itself offers no anonymity. The public ledger has a timeline of all funds moved. People trying to replace other transaction mechanisms with Bitcoin have to worry if the timing, quantities, frequency, and partners of Bitcoin trades could give the world enough information to target them for abuse or persecution. This isn't the only problem; law enforcement might be able to convince miners to refuse to do business with your Bitcoins. The Bitcoin system is not resilient to all kinds of attacks.

Monero is to Bitcoin as Tor is to the public internet. It uses a ring signature to allow people trying to transact to use each other's input transactions instead. The interaction between people is randomized and mostly one-way, decreasing the possible attack surface.

Monero fights the scalability effects on trust centralization due to mining pools in two ways. Monero doesn't allow for transaction fees to be set, instead making all blocks equally attractive to mine. This defeats a scaling issue which Bitcoin will face when the reward for mining will come entirely from transaction fees. Secondly they obfuscate transactions to protect miners from effective legal demands.

RESOURCES

https://en.Bitcoin.it/wiki/Main_Page

https://lightning.network/lightning-network-paper.pdf

https://getmonero.org/home

http://joel.mn/post/103546215249/the-blockchain-application-stack

https://21.co/learn/intro-to-micropayment-channels/#implementation-detailshttp://counterparty.io/platform/

https://gendal.me/2014/10/26/a-simple-explanation-of-Bitcoin-sidechains/

http://weuse.cash/ring-signatures/

Nakamoto S. (2008): Bitcoin: A peer-to-peer electronic cash system.
(http://www.Bitcoin.org/Bitcoin.pdf)

Chapter 5

HOW PEERCOIN WORKS

Consistency without the Energy Bill Through Proof Of Stake

INTRO

This week, we examine Peercoin. I'm not going to go into the threat model, because it has the same threat model as Bitcoin. It has a slightly different idea of what an "enemy" might be though.

In Bitcoin, we say that if an adversary has 51% of the mining power, then they win. The idea of one CPU giving you one vote is nice, but it ignores the fact that 51% of the mining power costs much less than 51% of the Bitcoins would. Investing in mining gear suddenly looks profitable for a wealthy adversary. Peercoin wants to avoid this incentive by making the age of held coins determine the power of a vote.

Peercoin also intends to be more environmentally friendly than Bitcoin. Bitcoin mining has come to draw significant power. If Bitcoin had to mine the blocks to push the transaction volume of a large payment card processor, it would require immense banks of ASICs hashing guessing every day. We'd see centralization in mining power as it became more and more expensive to mine. These few actors would be playing the game of crypto lottery to coordinate together without trusting each other. Some would say this is at best a waste of electricity, and at worse that it undermines the goals of Bitcoin.

Peercoin hopes to remove power and hardware as the consumed resource by making the external resource consumed into time itself. By relying on the stake of those holding coins in the network, Peercoin makes it expensive to act quickly and makes it difficult for any single identity to play too large a role in the system.

COIN AGE

The idea of coin age has been known since the early days of Bitcoin. Coin age is a measurement of the amount of currency held, multiplied by the time since it was attained. Since a transaction consumes all of the input, sending the remainder back to the spender, this is akin to a measurement of the time since the coin was last changed.

An attacker who wants to acquire coins rapidly will likely have a problem with steadily acquiring coin age. To keep $1,000 in spendable coin age every day, you would need to acquire $1,000 in coin every day. You could only recycle the coin after it had aged thirty days, upon which the coin age is destroyed when it's used.

Coin age is truly the vote of the old money then. Those with the longest holdings of a coin are those who have the most investment in its success, one reasons.

PROOF OF STAKE VIA COIN AGE

How does this coin age measurement allow one to implement a voting system for extending the blockchain?

Coin ages start being counted after the transaction making the coin amount is more than thirty days old. This has to do with checkpointing, as mentioned below. It allows nodes to deterministically agree on coin age through the checkpointing mechanism.

Peercoin has proof-of-work blocks, but most blocks won't be mined by proof-of-work. Proof-of-stake blocks will include a transaction in which the minter sends themselves their coins. These must have a coin age signifying they're greater than thirty days old.

Now this age goes into voting by acting as a "difficulty setting" for the hash target for a typical SHA-256, HashCash-style proof-of-work. This system allows someone spending more coin age to have the output of their hash-guess-lottery fall within a broader range and consider it success. This is probabilistically the same as giving the old money more lottery tickets for the same amount of money. After the work has been done, the worker needs to sign the block. This prevents the minter from using their same lowered difficulty to mine another block with the same parent. Nodes see the duplication and drop both, and the blockchain continues due to the signatures of honest nodes.

Peercoin further diverges from Bitcoin by creating a system which automatically scales the difficulty multiplier as the chain is built. In order to ensure that blocks are mined at an agreed-upon rate, the blocks contain a difficulty multiplier that can be adjusted. This continual changes allows the network to scale to sharp changes, in contrast with Bitcoin's periodic reassessments that can shock the mining economy.

Lastly, each transaction has a transaction fee which is destroyed. Furthermore, there are costs associated with everything that modifies the blockchain. This protects against attacks to fill the blockchain by making it expensive.

MINTING ECONOMICS

Minting is perhaps much less lucrative in Peercoin. There is a 1% return annually on the amount of coin that someone puts toward minting. It's not even guaranteed to be a profit. If two people mint the same block in a given timeframe, the one with the most coin age will win. When a transaction stakes it's coins, they are locked for 520 block confirmations over three to four days. These minting coins can't be used for day-to-day transactions, they have to be set aside. Merging transactions, spending them, or doing anything really will cause coin age to reset to zero. Minting more frequently doesn't even get you more. If you mint every thirty days, you'll be expected to make the same amount as if you minted annually.

Minting, unlike Bitcoin mining, is not like striking gold. Minting is akin to taking in your cash every now and then and asking to have it "upgraded" to account for inflation. This keeps people invested in the system, and keeps the power out of the hands of any one group of people. Lastly, it makes it unprofitable for someone to make a run on the system by making it expensive to mine multiple blocks. This makes attacks more expensive than the Bitcoin network, as long as it remains expensive to buy most Peercoin.

RESOURCES

King S. and Nadal S. (2012): PPCoin: Peer-to-Peer Crypto-Currency with Proof-of-Stake (http://www.peercoin.net/assets/paper/peercoin-paper.pdf)

Chapter 6

HOW NAMECOIN WORKS

An Internet We Can Agree On: Secured DNS through The Blockchain

INTRO

The Internet is peculiar place. People will tell you that it is the first thing of value truly owned by everybody and nobody collectively. This could not be farther from the truth. We do not own the Internet because we do not own the means of coordination.

While the internet is ostensibly a swarm of nameless CPUs with network interfaces, playing IP address roulette is outside the scope of anybody's time. We rely on DNS, which means that we rely on the goodwill of the government of the United States to continue to run ICANN in a non-hostile manner. This trust has been violated numerous times; website domain names have been seized and the sites redirected to an image reading "This domain name has been seized by ICE--Homeland Security Investigations, pursuant to a seizure warrant issued by a United States District Court."

Furthermore, the security of server public key distribution has become a joke that stopped being funny a long time ago. When you visit a website, you're given a chain of certificates. Each certificate proves that an entity trusts the site, and the end of the chain is somebody that you trust absolutely. The problem with this absolute trust is that it is violated quite regularly. Legal pressures and financial incentives have made these authorities give out duplicate certificates in the past such that impersonation becomes practical. We can only expect more and more such demands.
[https://www.schneier.com/academic/archives/2000/01/ten_risks_of_pki_wha.html]

If the bedrock of the HTTPS-driven Internet is not safe from bad actors, then the entire system is compromised. Most of the major sites you visit have had attacks attempted on them at one time or another in this vein. It's only a matter of time before warrantless SSL-wiretaps become a thing, potentially with malware on the other side of that transmission.

Namecoin wants to put the DNS and CA system into the hands of the Internet itself by storing the state on an alternate blockchain that manages to borrow the work of Bitcoin mining without sacrificing security.

THREAT MODEL

The threat model of Namecoin is very much like the threat model of Bitcoin, with a few specific differences. The network will be eventually consistent with a linear ordering, where state changes become cryptographically intractable to alter after their blocks have become farther back in the blockchain. Due to the use of Namecoin for identity manipulation, there are extra attacks to worry about.

If an attacker sees you trying to put a block into the network that registers "myMillionDollarName," then they could decide that they want this name instead. They might want to sell it back to you at a high price. Namecoin solves this by separating the registration process into two steps. At first, the user inserts a block into the network that contains only the hash of the name that you want. After this hash is in a block at least 12 blocks away from the newest mined block, Namecoin will allow you to submit a "first update" transaction that exposes the actual name and information. Future updates can be made to change where the address points, and to renew it before it expires.

What if an attacker wants to register all alphanumeric names, and become the new ICANN by selling them to you at a steep premium and under a strict contract. This becomes very difficult. An attacker must spend money on the registration transaction fee, but must also spend money on a registration fee when they send their first "block registration" block. This registration fee is destroyed, it cannot be somehow revived and reused by anybody. There are no registration fees for renewals or updates, but a transaction fee does apply. You have to renew or update a name every 35,999 blocks at the latest (between 200 and 250 days), otherwise it expires. This makes holding on to a lot of domains expensive.

On the other hand, Namecoin offers no protection against squatting. A squatter can register "google" and demand a ransom when Google decides to get a Namecoin address. There's not much one can do here without requiring out-of-bound validation, which some would consider an attack on the network itself.

ARCHITECTURE

Namecoin is currently a naming system with two namespaces. One of them is for the identities of people, while the other is for the identities of software systems.

Identities for people consist of a mapping between usernames and contact information for that identity. The GPG fingerprint can be included in this chain to act as a key registry for email transmission, though the actual keys are not stored to conserve space.

Domain names are really a key-value store between a string key and a set of attributes that allows someone to interact with the computer behind the domain. This is exactly how Namecoin works. The value is a lot more rich than DNS currently allows. It can register a user, an IP address, an IPv6 address, a Tor hidden service address, an I2P address, a Freenet address, an owner email address, geographic locations for the hosting, a DNS name server to forward the lookup to, a key-value store for the locations of subdomains, a fingerprint of a TLS certificate, and a set of round-robin IP addresses to route to for load balancing. These are not disjoint choices, most of these can be placed in the same Namecoin value body and the user can choose how to use the information.

Actual interaction works currently by having the local Namecoin client act as a DNS server and as a CA authority. It will expose these to the machine, while pulling the necessary data from the blockchain.

TLS works fairly simply, where the name points to a TLS certificate fingerprint. The website on the other end of the network socket will serve up the certificate as part of the handshake, and it can be validated against the blockchain rather than against your government's database.

MERGED MINING

The strength of any blockchain-based technology depends entirely on the number of users the network has. When a blockchain has too few good users, it becomes cheap for an attacker to coordinate enough resources to rewrite history by altering previous blocks and outracing the rest of the network. If Namecoin had used a separate mining population for its separate blockchain, it would have ran up against these problems.

The solution is called merged mining. The size of a block and the difficulty of mining the block are a heuristic tradeoff between history immutability and throughput. Let's say that currently a powerful attacker can rewrite history quickly enough to change the last three blocks. If it tried the last four, it wouldn't be able to catch up before the network started making more blocks and made it intractable for the attacker. If the block size got larger or the work got easier, then an attacker could reverse more transactions.

However, merged mining allows Namecoin to securely get the Bitcoin mining population to mine two blocks at once by making them heterogeneous. Rewriting one Bitcoin block allows an attacker to rewrite one Namecoin block. Since the difficulty rates for information are similar as before, Namecoin can trust blocks that are old enough in the Bitcoin blockchain.

Whenever Namecoin has enough transactions to mine a block, it will insert the hash into a field of a Bitcoin transaction that does not invalidate the transaction, and will have this transaction mined for a standard transaction fee. When this block is mined, the Bitcoin blockchain contains proof-of-work for the Namecoin block. The Namecoin blockchain will now insert this Bitcoin block into the Namecoin blockchain, dropping everything in the Merkle tree not necessary to validate the single mined transaction (to keep the Namecoin blockchain small). This serves as a proof-of-work for Namecoin.

USE OF THE NAMECOIN BLOCKCHAIN

BY OTHER APPLICATIONS

Namecoin offers features that may be attractive for other applications. Management of server and person identities is paramount in many computer systems. The promise of a simple, global, shared, auditable user identity system is attractive for many reasons. Namecoin requires a minor fee to register an account, making spamming or denial of service financially unreasonable for an attacker. In fact, we see nameID (openID provider) and bitMessage (chat) use Namecoin for just these purposes.

When thinking of storing more complex information in the blockchain, one must be weary. Namecoin has some performance problems which arise from the nature of blockchain consistency. Each record is limited to 520 bytes, which may not be enough for systems which want to store complex information. Likewise, it is neither low-latency nor free. A block is mined every 10 minutes, and requires a Namecoin transaction fee to be paid to miners. It isn't reasonable to use it as a distributed file system, and will not become a global SQL database any time soon.

But there really isn't a problem with this. If you're trying to store all of the state of your application in the blockchain, you're doing something wrong. Namecoin is an example of a more general usage of blockchains which offers a lot of promise. Consider an RSS feed of weather monitor updates. Every time it wants to update the reading, it places this data in a data structure that is replicated via a DHT or over the BitTorrent network. Now you can store torrent hashes in Namecoin, or you can place torrent hashes in a data structure in the network, and you can put that hash in the network.

Like most things in Computer Science, many problems with using blockchains as a component of a larger system can be solved with another level of indirection.

RESOURCES

https://nameid.org/

https://bitmessage.org/wiki/Main_Page

https://github.com/namecoin/namecoin-legacy/blob/namecoinq/DESIGN-namecoin.md

https://wiki.namecoin.org/index.php?title=Identity

https://wiki.namecoin.org/index.php?title=Domain_Name_Specification

Chapter 7

HOW ZEROCASH WORKS

Privacy on the Blockchain

INTRO

ZeroCash is to Bitcoin like Tor is to network traffic. Bitcoin's dirty little secret is that it has very little privacy; anybody who reads the chain can figure out what accounts are doing. By following the flow of money, an adversary can spy on a person's monetary activities. ZeroCash pools assets in order to get privacy.

Increasingly worrying is the lack of forward secrecy on the blockchain. There's nothing to stop a heavy-handed agency from subpoenaing everybody who sent someone Bitcoin. Someone can be found guilty through association. Scarier to some than a court of law, Bitcoin transactions may make someone a target to another party. Hacktivists and simple hackers will know who has a fortune in Bitcoin and might be motivated to attack one's computer to get access to the keys for the Bitcoins.

Many people turn to sites called tumblers. Tumblers are centralized sites that take in Bitcoin and allow users to "cash out" Bitcoin. This works to split a Bitcoin wallet up into hundreds of pieces and to give a different hundred pieces to a different Bitcoin account. This policy is currently the standard way to get privacy with Bitcoin. This way is not perfect though.

This centralized tumbler might act in bad faith. They might act good for 99 days and on the 100th day run off with thousands of dollars in Bitcoin. They might be working with an attacker to profile transactions. They may take your hundred Bitcoins and give them all to somebody who uses them to break the law in a way that traces back to you. They may do all of these at the same time.

ZeroCash is a protocol underlying the newer tumbler pool called ZCash that hopes to provide a trustless solution to tumbling.

IMPLEMENTATION

The basic idea behind ZeroCash is to create a pool of funds that anybody can use to mix their holdings in. After adding one's Bitcoins to the pool, one can take out an equal amount of other Bitcoins in order to hide the paper trail. The problem with this is that the process of identifying which deposit the withdrawing user had used is enough information to identify the withdrawing user. This could defeat the purpose. ZeroCash thus uses zero-knowledge proofs to check and manipulate people's balances without exposing which balances are being manipulated.

ZeroCash has a construction which uses some tools that we haven't seen before. ZeroCash falls back upon non-interactive zero-knowledge proofs (zk-SNARKs). These are slower than some of the other cryptography that we've seen before. These zk-SNARKs are quite complex things. They enable someone to validate certain characteristics about a piece of encrypted data without seeing the decrypted data. The crazy thing is that in ZeroCash, this zero-knowledge proof will provide evidence that someone has been owed enough

ZeroCash has two operations, Mix and Pour. Both of them build up the cryptographic state to create a new "now." When someone adds new coins to the pool, they perform a Mix. When someone removes coins from their pool, they perform a Pour.

Since it's relatively expensive to use the zk-SNARK, most of ZeroCash's design is based around minimizing the amount of reliance on the mechanism. Mix and Pour both create states to validate, but only Pour transactions really require a full validation as Pour transactions are the only ones that require action from the pool. These transactions are a few microseconds, so they're not incredibly slow. They would definitely pose a problem to scaling to a proof on every Bitcoin transaction.

One of the secrets to scaling ZeroCash is that the zk-SNARK is not forced to handle a structure tracking every account in the pool. ZeroCash maintains a Merkle tree. The depth of the tree is logarithmic in the number of transactions, making it much more computationally tractable to carry out the slower zk-SNARK operations.

EFFECTIVENESS

ZeroCash is just fast enough to do what it promises but too slow to do much more. The algorithm underlying the system is quite powerful and complex, using cryptographically-verified manipulation of ledgers that nobody can read the entirety of. People interact with the ledger to carry out their ZeroCash activities, creating a state that can be queried and verified later.

Nowhere in this state is there a decrypted copy of whom has inserted and removed the coins in question. When someone wishes to remove a unit of currency from the system, they cause the state to change in a way that does this without exposing their role in the operation. This offers near perfect anonymity to the user.

The problem is that this system is both very powerful and fairly slow. While only taking milliseconds to verify a number of proofs, these add up. This means that most people won't use ZeroCash between every transaction, only as a way to "clean" a quantity of coins of a paper trail.

This nature is reinforced more by the fact that ZeroCash is unsuitable for transactions. Transactions require a long chain of money changing hands; which may become arbitrarily difficult to process. Because of this, and because of the lack of ZeroCash proof checking by Bitcoin miners, ZeroCash cannot work as a sidechain and transfer money between peers. ZeroCash is only a money tumbling service.

How good of a money tumbling service is it? So no longer can a tumbler operator collect traffic analysis or steal from a user. No longer does Bitcoin laundering require communication with multiple active parties.

On the other hand, someone who analyzes the ZeroCash network may be able to perform attacks which are quite similar to the attacks on any mix network. If an attacker observed someone pay 0.083 Bitcoins to ZeroCash and then 0.083 Bitcoins in transactions leaving the network and all eventually going to the same address, then the attacker can correlate the message. Likewise, if someone uses the network for a quick Mix and Pour in the middle of the night when the network has few other people, then the timing of the transaction is enough to betray who was doing the mixing. Lastly, you have no control what the coins that you put into the pool are doing. You may be unintentionally implicating your Bitcoins in felonies.

ZeroNet thus needs enough users for "privacy in numbers" in order to get real privacy.

EXTENSIONS OF IDEA

The really interesting thing is to consider the mechanics of this system. By anonymously allowing users to "check in" and "check out" resources from a global pool, ZeroCash contributes a novel cryptographic technique. In many systems, embedded devices will take and return resources such as shared locks. These systems must work hard to prevent reverse engineering and obfuscation.

ZeroCash seems like a reliable model for cooperative resource sharing among agents with strong ownership. After it becomes more mainstream, it will be interesting to see how it may be applied to the embedded blockchain domain.

RESOURCES

https://github.com/scipr-lab/libsnark

http://zerocash-project.org/media/pdf/zerocash-oakland2014.pdf

http://eprint.iacr.org/2013/879

https://z.cash/

Chapter 8

HOW ETHEREUM WORKS

Verified Code Execution Through the Blockchain

INTRO

Software is incredibly powerful. Like most things in mathematics, the more powerful the thing being studied is, the harder it is to state useful things about it. In fact, the definition of programming as we know it came from Turing's seminal paper on the Halting Problem which told us what we couldn't do with a computer. It is from this that we draw the name "Turing-complete" to describe any system which is computationally powerful enough to run into the same limitations.

The Halting problem prevents us from knowing for sure how a computation will turn out without running. A slightly different problem that haunts many domains is that software is inherently disappearing. In calling a function, we trade the arguments for the end result. In the name of space efficiency, we later discard our arguments most of the time. At some point a variable is "useless" and the data it contained is erased.

Anybody who has gotten a bug report with an application state that seems borderline nonsense can understand the pain of this. Trying to reverse-engineer what one's own code did is what makes debugging so time consuming.

A slightly different problem caused by this is that it becomes important where code is run. When two systems cooperatively interact to compute something, something can go wrong at every single step of the way. Frequently, something does. It becomes the duty of an ultimately trusted entity to pick up the pieces and decide what the correct view of the world should be. In many situations, this is unacceptable.

THE SOLUTION

Ethereum tries to solve this problem by having everybody run the code, and by keeping around the arguments used to generate the result indefinitely. If this sounds expensive, it is. Someone using Ethereum to do numerical computation over a large amount of data is going to have to pay the network a lot for it.

Most applications aren't like this though. Most applications are thin, pretty wrappers around a data store that allow for simplistic manipulation. Messaging applications, commerce, social networks, and asset management applications are all examples of this.

The interesting thing is that when everybody is running the code, it is almost as if nobody is running the code. There's no need to keep servers online constantly to receive messages that might come with unknown frequency. The network as a whole provides uptime on behalf of the application writer. In this way, Ethereum applications are frequently called "serverless."

Ethereum promises a lot, and they do a pretty good job of delivering on it.

ARCHITECTURE

Ethereum is a blockchain technology, like many of the architectures that we've covered thus far. Human input into the network is done by sending transactions to the mining pool, which validates the transaction and adds it to a block to mine. After a miner manages to find the integer necessary to make the block's hash smaller than a determined difficulty, the block is considered part of the chain and the mining pool starts on the next block.

In financial blockchains, a transaction is always an exchange of value. Validating a transaction is thus validating that the person sending the money actually has the money. Bitcoin also has a scripting language which allows for very rudimentary computation. In Ethereum, use of the scripting language is the primary reason to use the network. Ethereum also contains a currency, which is used primarily to pay the transaction fee to the miners but can be sent between people as well. Validating an Ethereum transaction involves executing scripts held by the recipient of a transaction, which is paid for with the sender's transaction currency.

CONTRACTS

A contract is born by making a transaction which contains the compiled code of a contract in the data field. After mining, this contract becomes an entity that can receive transactions.

A contract is really thought of as a self-contained piece of code that responds to payment messages by executing the script. This script execution can essentially do anything that a person interacting with Ethereum can do. Scripts can create new contracts, send transactions to other contracts, and save the results of computation to a permanent storage. Anything that requires computation or storage has a computational fee that is measured in "gas" and is what determines the mining fee.

What's interesting is that these Turing complete virtual machines live on the blockchain to serve their defined goals without any further need for the code author to interact with the network. As long as the people who need to run the code can afford the execution, the network will take care of everything.

MANAGING

TURING COMPLETENESS

WITH GAS MONEY

Now anybody familiar with the Halting problem will flinch at the thought of putting an open server out there which will run any code submitted to it. An infinite loop can be crafted to lock up a system. A malicious agent would be able to derail every node that tries to validate that transaction.

Ethereum handles this through fine-grained accounting. A transaction contains two figures that determine the cost to the sender. The STARTGAS counts the computational load of operations that the sender expects the contract to run. Operations which store data or are more computationally expensive have a higher price in gas. The GASPRICE is the rate that the sender is willing to pay per "gas" unit in terms of Ethereum's underlying currency.

A transaction verifier will run a contract until the gas runs out, or until the script finishes. If the script finishes then the remaining gas is refunded to the recipient and the miner keeps the product of the consumed gas and GASPRICE. If the gas runs out, all state changes are reverted and the miner just keeps the money.

SCALABILITY

Ethereum, like Bitcoin, faces the issue of storage. If Bitcoin were to handle the load of a modern credit card processing company, it would grow by about 1GB per hour. If Ethereum were to become mainstream, a naive implementation of it might face the same issues. As the blockchain grows, fewer and fewer nodes can afford to hold onto the entire chain. These "full nodes" have all of the power; if they were to form a malicious alliance then the history of the blockchain would be at risk.

Ethereum will likely scale a bit easier by the fact that the blockchain is not quite necessary to get a full view of the state of the network. Each Ethereum full node needs only to hold onto the global storage and the holdings of accounts, and can fold each incoming block into this.

Ethereum uses a modification of a Merkle tree optimized for addition and removal called a Patricia tree. This tree refers to subtrees of previous blocks by hash and tries to reduce hash invalidation. This is used to create a hash of the global application state that can be inserted into each block.

Ethereum has a formal method for finding the bad link in a poisoned chain. If a chain has a defect, it must occur between two blocks such that state N is correct and state N+1 is not. By walking through the blockchain from an expected good state, maybe even the initial block, a node can find the exact wrong state transition and can offer it to the network as proof that another miner had mined a bad block.

There is another kind of scalability worth considering, and that's the ability to do things cheaply. Ethereum's costs are relatively high currently, making it inappropriate for certain classes of high-throughput systems. Ethereum is moving to proof-of-stake in order to make it less computationally costly to mine, and therefore less expensive for the end user to run contracts.

THE DAO

One cannot talk about Ethereum without talking about the problem that was the DAO. The DAO, or distributed autonomous organization, was an entity that would hold the users' funds in a joint account that would be utilized as the holders saw fit.

The DAO was widely successful, raising $150 Million.

Unfortunately, the contract behind the DAO had a few bugs. Furthermore, the creators of the project didn't expect such a success, and put all of the money into a single account. This enabled an attacker to leave the DAO in a state that threatened to have the funds made useless or able to be stolen outright.

The solution that the Ethereum project saw was to provide miners with an option to choose to continue mining the version of the blockchain that contained the result of the DAO and the attacker's actions, or to mine a new version that relocated the funds so that caretakers of the DAO could refund those who bought in to the best of their ability.

The miners favored the refund, and the attacker had their funds taken from them by the network. This "hard fork" was met with both relief and unease. This showed that unpopular actors in a blockchain network can have the network decide to do whatever it wants with their funds. While this is no surprise, given the nature of the 51% attack vulnerability in blockchains, it burst the bubble of some of the most crypto-anarchist-libertarian supporters of cryptocurrency.

Cryptocurrency assets are able to be seized. The global consensus of ownership is a democracy due to the nature of the underlying blockchain.

ETHEREUM ECOSYSTEM

A language or virtual machine succeeds or fails based on the flexibility of implementations and the availability of existing libraries. Ethereum is no different. There are many programmatic implementations of the clients currently, but the exciting stuff is still on the horizon.

At this point in time, much effort is being put into Ethereum's Mist browser. Mist offers a user-friendly interface for the intricacies of distributed serverless applications. It functions as a client for the Ethereum network and prioritizes privacy and the user experience.

I look forward to seeing the distributed applications that people will build for this exciting new platform.

REFERENCES

https://github.com/ethereum/wiki/wiki/White-Paper

https://github.com/ethereum/wiki/wiki/Mining

http://ethdocs.org/en/latest

https://blog.ethereum.org/2016/07/12/build-server-less-applications-mist/

https://github.com/ethereum/mist

http://www.coindesk.com/understanding-dao-hack-journalists/

Chapter 9

HOW TEXTSECURE WORKS

The Method Of Secure Chat on Signal, WhatsApp, Facebook, and More

INTRO

The goal of TextSecure is to offer "end-to-end security, deniability, forward secrecy, and future secrecy". What this means in practice is that TextSecure wants to construct a stream of messages between two people which keeps key material around for as short a time as possible. Key compromise in the future should not make it possible to decrypt traffic observed today.

I've covered a critical analysis of the Signal Protocol below. It studies the implemented architecture, notes discovered flaws, and evaluates how well the stated goals are met. A deeper analysis of the goals follows the system description.

TERMINOLOGY

TextSecure is one name given to the application now called Signal. The codebase and the documentation throughout it use the name TextSecure. In order to maintain consistency with the System, I will refer to the entire system as TextSecure.

In reality, there are a number of different things here:

The TextSecure Server, referred to as TS in the linked whitepapers (bottom) is the centralized server which coordinates state for the rest of the system.

The Signal Protocol refers to the more general protocol in use by messaging apps from Facebook Messenger to Google Allo. It implements the functionality described below, but leaves these implementations free to do message routing and metadata tracking however they like.

The Signal application is a mobile application which implements the Signal Protocol using the described TextSecure Server policies analyzed below. This is the original implementation of the protocol.

ARCHITECTURE

TextSecure is a modification of the Off-The-Record chat protocol with a focus on asynchronous coordination. Whereas OTR requires an interactive handshake, TextSecure considers the indeterminate latency unacceptable. Having to bring an app into the foreground and carry out a handshake before being able to send a message would offer a terrible user experience.

Instead, copies of the server's role in the key negotiation are stored by a centralized server for potential clients to fetch and use. This server acts as a channel not trusted with key information able to decrypt anything; all encryption is end to end.

CRYPTOGRAPHY

TextSecure uses a small set of cryptographic primitives. Public key cryptography is carried out through elliptic-curve Diffie-Hellman using Curve25519. AES is used for symmetric encryption, for both counter mode without padding and cipher block chaining mode. HMAC-SHA256 is used for message authentication. These are the trusted base.

DOUBLE RATCHET

The core of TextSecure's encryption engine is the Axolotl double ratchet algorithm. The big-picture idea is that there are two ratchets that can move forward: a receive ratchet and a send ratchet. The structure allows for the first half of the key negotiation to be saved and replayed asynchronously later to yield a full handshake.

The receive ratchet is used when a message is received, which must include new material for the next key negotiation. This material is used to generate new symmetric keys for encryption and message authentication later.

The sending hash ratchet generates a new set of keys using the keystream generated from the previous set of coordinated shared secrets. This ratchet is reset when the receive ratchet is activated and the shared secrets change.

What is important here to observe is that a sender never has to wait in order to send a message. They can always take a step to send a message which terminates in a bounded amount of time. These messages will all be encrypted with different symmetric keys. This means that the current keys on either person's devices cannot be used to decrypt a message sent in the past. (We see later that this has one caveat.)

PROTOCOL

Phase 1: TextSecure Registration

Registration starts by having a client tell the server the phone number with which it can be contacted, as well as whether it would prefer to receive a token via phone call or via SMS. This token acts as the proof of ownership which enables the user to store registration information with TextSecure.

The client sends message authentication and

encryption symmetric keys ('signaling' keys), and their long-term public key.

It also posts a collection of prekeys, which are one-time copies of the client's half of key negotiation when the client is a recipient. These stored prekeys allow a sender to carry out key negotiation without requiring the client be able to respond, reducing negotiation latency significantly. The client also uploads a "prekey of last resort" which is used last and is shared between all sessions until the recipient pushes new prekeys.

That signal doesn't warn the user about relying on a prekey that's been used by other clients is less than ideal, in my opinion.

The client then registers with Google Cloud Messaging to get a registration ID to give TextSecure. This registration with TextSecure includes whether the client wants to receive SMS or only data.

Phase 2: Key Comparison

TextSecure allows for clients to compare the fingerprint of each other's long-term keys to verify each other's identity. It also includes support for displaying keys as QR codes to enable convenient comparison.

Phase 3.1: Sending an Initial Message

The sender starts by requesting a prekey for the recipient. They're given the prekey index, the prekey, the registration ID, and the long-term public key of the recipient. These are used to negotiate a shared secret through the HDKF key derivation algorithm. This is referred to as the root key.

An ephemeral key pair is generated for this message. The root key is used with HDKF to derive a new root key and a chaining key. This chaining key is what is used to generate encryption and MAC keys.

Lastly, AES counters are initialized. There are two counters: ctr and pctr. The ctr counter is incremented with every sent message while the pctr counter holds the counter of the last message seen. This allows a recipient to enforce an ordering between messages received out of order.

These are used to encrypt the message for the recipient, which is send to the signal server. This message contains the information necessary for the recipient to complete the key negotiation handshake.

The signal server will check that the Google Cloud Messenger registration ID is right for the phone number in question, and will encrypt the message with the 'signaling' keys before sending the message to the cloud server. This indirection ensures that Google Cloud Messenger does not see the message sender.

Phase 3.2: Receiving a Message

The sender receives the prekey index and uses it to find the prekey used by the sender. It then uses the information sent to complete the handshake and to find the same root keys as the sender. These generate the keys used to decrypt the sent message.

Phase 4: Sending a Follow-up Message

If the original sender wants to send a second

message before the recipient replies, they generate a new chaining key and use this to find new encryption and message authentication keys.

Phase 5: Sending a Reply

When the recipient wishes to reply they first choose a new ephemeral key pair. Using the sender's ephemeral public key, and their ephemeral private key, they generate a new shared secret. This is used to find a new chaining key to find new keys for encryption and authorization. This is used to encrypt the message, which is sent along with the new ephemeral public key.

KNOWN ISSUES

Key Submission

TextSecure uses a shared secret between the TextSecure server and client, the machine-generated "pw", to authenticate upload of new prekeys. This is also used for authenticating sent messages. Leaking the password is then enough to allow someone to both send messages and upload keys on behalf of a user. The encrypted export function allowed a TextSecure client to move accounts between phones, but was removed because the export included the machine-generated password in it. This unencrypted backup was placed on the device's SD card, which meant that other apps on the phone could read it.

This feature has since been removed. If you noticed it missing, it's not a usability bug. It's a conservative approach to a real problem.

Unknown Key-Share Attack

This attack is one of forged delivery. If an attacker carries out a UKS attack, they trick someone into crafting a message for another person (the target) when they believe they are communicating with the attacker.

This is easily done by a powerful attacker by replacing their own public key on the TextSecure server with the target's public key. They can do this by re-registering their number with TextSecure. They then can use QR codes to validate that their fingerprint matches what the sender has. This is the fingerprint of the target's key.

Then, they must re-register the sender's account and intercept the validation SMS or phone call from reaching the sender. This is trivial to anybody with a permissive-enough warrant. They now can authenticate as the sender and pass along the signed message.

This attack has not been fixed by TextSecure. They added signing of prekeys, but they are still not cryptographically associated with an identity. They may be passed-off and replayed due to this lack of association.

A feasible fix would be to have the sender and recipient both mentioned in the encrypted body of the message.

GOAL EVALUATION

TextSecure achieves forward security due to its construction. Forward secrecy states that if long-lived public keys remain secure, that leakage of current symmetric keys forms a security breach which is active for a bounded amount of time. Since the public keys are required in each new ratchet, this is met.

Perfect forward secrecy is defined as the property that seizing the current keys had by a client won't allow an adversary from decrypting messages sent previously. This is enforced by the TextSecure wire protocol but it turns into a bit of a semantics game. Since keys are only stored on the devices, it is unlikely for a key to be disclosed without having access to other keys currently on the app. The long-term key isn't enough to decrypt a message without the short-term keys associated with the ratchet state, but these can be pulled from the phone and used to decrypt messages sent and not yet replied to (messages using the previous ratchet). This is disclosure of a "previous" message technically.

Deniability is much shaker. While it's possible to say that anybody could have created a given message, since the prekeys are published, the centralization of TextSecure poses a threat to that. The TextSecure server authenticates and forwards messages, and may log them. While the content is encrypted end-to-end, the metadata is not.

RESOURCES

Tilman Frosch ; Christian Mainka ; Christoph Bader ; Florian Bergsma ; Jörg Schwenk ; Thorsten Holz (12 May 2016). "How Secure is TextSecure?". Retrieved November 27 2016. (http://ieeexplore.ieee.org/document/7467371/)

Marlinspike, Moxie (30 March 2016). "Signal on the outside, Signal on the inside". Open Whisper Systems. Retrieved 31 March 2016.

Chapter 10

HOW BITTORRENT WORKS

Survival Through Full Distribution

INTRO

BitTorrent is both ambitious and simple. BitTorrent is a P2P protocol in which peers coordinate to distribute requested files. In order to resist downtime due to real-world seizure of computers, BitTorrent has had to progress to a fully distributed architecture, without any single point of failure. This is an impressive technical feat.

Even more impressive is that BitTorrent gets faster with additional content-fetchers, rather than slower. The classic economics of content distribution is suddenly inverted, rewarding high-desirability content.

It's no surprise then that BitTorrent is used nowadays for everything from sharing Linux ISO files to live broadcast streaming of sports and politics. BitTorrent's name is still controversial in many places because of its role as a subversive software. BitTorrent's power made it the first choice for piracy, which lead to many concluding that BitTorrent is only useful for piracy. While many ISPs and externally-administered networks attempt to block and trace BitTorrent, the fight has largely been lost.

By not placing restrictions on peers, BitTorrent opens itself up to a universe of attacks. Like other architectures, a combination of limited observability and sound mathematics is the solution. As we will see, the architecture prevents an evil actor from serving a corrupted file or causing undue load on the BitTorrent network.

Lastly, BitTorrent is forward-thinking. It contains an extension protocol that allows clients to design protocols that alter the behavior of peers, and enables peers to intelligently fall back upon the extensions supported by each. At the bottom of this is the basic peer protocol; ensuring that clients can agree on enough to simply serve the file if they share no extensions.

THE PEER PROTOCOL

When a peer wants to start sharing a file, they construct a metadata file that describes the attributes of the file as well as a number of options. BitTorrent uses bencoding for most data sent, which prefixes a data literal with a character describing its type and its length (if a string). The metadata will describe the files in the torrent, but also includes a SHA1 hash of each of the "pieces" or file fragments in the torrent. These fragments can be downloaded individually, allowing for streaming or for selective downloading.

The file's attributes are known as the "info" block and is what uniquely defines the torrent. The info block's hash is the torrent's unique identifier in the BitTorrent swarm of peers. This metadata file also announces a tracker that the torrent will be associated with. This is outside of the info block, to enable multiple tracker to track the same torrent and to have the same infohash.

This metadata file is half of what a downloader needs to know to download the file. The other half is the list of peers serving the torrent. Conventionally, a peer will query the torrent tracker for a list of peers serving the file. The distributed hash table, peer exchange, and local service discovery are all other methods. We will discuss the first later. The latter two can be thought of as "gossip" protocol extensions that allow peers to become known by the swarm.

Now once a peer has a list of peers, and has connected to each of them over TCP (or the uTorrent transport protocol, not covered here), it now uses the peer protocol to fetch all of the files. These peer connections are bidirectional and have attributes set on them by either side. Peers will announce when they have finished downloading a piece, so that peers connected to them know whether they want anything from a certain peer.

A side may be interested, which means that they want "pieces" that the other peer has. A side may also be choking, which means that they're busy sharing with another peer. When a connection is both interested and unchoked, then data transmission happens. Peers will use "optimistic unchoking," or rotation of the choke list, to ensure that there is enough choke variability for the swarm to have a fair chance of progressing. Choking is done in order to limit the number of outbound TCP connections, to ensure that the communication switching overhead is low enough for a peer to be useful to those it is connected to.

Transmission only occurs when one side is interested and the other side is not choking. This enables peers to have a tit-for-tat where the peers which share the most freely are the ones which are able to access pieces the most rapidly. This localized enforcement of good behavior enables the network to scale upwards without collapsing. The hashing of all pieces sent ensure that no peers can "poison" the network by sending bad file fragments. This pervasive integrity checking was one of the things that allowed BitTorrent to succeed where its early competitors failed.

DHT AND MAGNET LINKS

BitTorrent uses a DHT protocol to enable peer discovery without requiring communication with the centralized tracker. DHT "nodes" are not the same thing as torrent "peers," although a computer can be both. Nodes listen for DHT requests over UDP, while peers listen for the BitTorrent peer protocol over TCP. BitTorrent clients include a DHT node, which operates mostly as a querying "client" node.

The Kademlia-like DHT works by giving each DHT node an ID. IDs have a "closeness" metric that is computed by XORing two IDs together and interpreting the result as an unsigned integer. Nodes will know about other nodes which have a low XOR distance and will know about few nodes that have a high XOR distance.

A client makes a query for a torrent by using the hash of the metadata's info as an ID, and finding the node that it knows that is closest to the key. This node is then sent the request. If the node doesn't have the torrent, the node forwards the request to the node that is the closest to the ID that it knows. This process iteratively finds the node in the network that is the closest to the query's key. If the peer can't find a peer tracking the metadata's info hash, it will have to insert itself as the node responsible for the key into the DHT by introducing itself to the nodes closest to the key.

In order to prevent a bad actor from registering other peers for torrents, the DHT includes a paper trail. The query will return a token. If the query fails, this token must be presented by the peer trying to register itself as responsible for the key. Tokens are only valid for approximately ten minutes.

A node constructs a list of peers by searching the DHT for nodes closest to its own node ID. Most of the peers the node knows will have nearly keys. A few exceptions will exist because of other observed nodes through other network operations. In this way, nodes tend to construct a very "localized" view of the network that makes it faster to narrow in on a single key quickly.

Now this DHT is quite simple, it associates peers with a torrent. In order to get the querying node enough information to begin downloading the torrent, the network must serve the torrent's metadata file as well. This newer feature is referred to as a "magnet" link, and enables a peer to complete an entire download using only the node ID. Trackers using magnet links need only provide links with hashes, rather than indexing and serving a collection of torrent metadata files.

PRIVATE TORRENTS

BitTorrent is a very inclusive network in its default state. The Distributed Hash Table, peer exchange, and local service discovery can all help a peer find other peers without having to rely on the tracker. While this is typically a good thing, it can be undesirable to remove the ability to control file distribution centrally.

One frequent use case for centralized control is to enforce a share ratio. When a community shares many files, it becomes important to enforce that peers upload an acceptable ratio of data to what they download.

This fine-grained access control is done by restricting peer information querying to those peers that the private tracker decides should be able to download the file. This is really security through obscurity.

"Once an intruder peer has obtained the IP address and port of a peer, regardless of the source, the intruder can initiate a connection to that peer and trade pieces with the peer. Once in the swarm, the intruder is granted equal treatment as all other peers."

Source: http://www.BitTorrent.org/beps/bep_0027.html

What happens is that the torrent's metadata file includes a "private" flag that tells peers to only use the tracker to exchange peers. Furthermore, a client may only use the peers from a single private tracker at a given time for a given torrent. This prevents a peer from uploading a private metadata file to a public tracker and having the existing swarm serve the file.

FUTURE

We're seeing a lot of new innovation in the BitTorrent sphere recently.

BitTorrent's power is proportional to its convenience. The associations with piracy have led to BitTorrent software that requires that one jump through a lot of hoops in order to use the software sometimes. You can only download from BitTorrent what peers are seeding through BitTorrent. Convenience is largely the reason that many consumers have abandoned piracy torrents in exchange for services like Netflix and Spotify.

PopcornTime (https://popcorntime.sh/) is an example of the power of BitTorrent with good content indexing and a nice UI. While it is plagued by the fact that it is a piracy-focused tool, PopcornTime represents a fairly flexible CDN system for popular media. One can imagine clones for open-access media and for news. What's worth noting is that the cost of running PopcornTime is absolutely minuscule for the software creators, especially compared to the behemoth infrastructure of Netflix. With good copy protection on media, BitTorrent may one day be seen as the powerful content-agnostic technology that it is.

BitTorrent is useful for a lot more than shuffling around large files though. WebTorrent uses the newer WebRTC browser features which enable P2P data channels. Browsers are now able to act as peers, making the ecosystem much more flexible. It's worth noting that WebTorrent peers are not compatible with BitTorrent peers due to the use of WebRTC for transport, rather than naked TCP sockets. As well as serving large media files, torrents can now serve static websites. Peers can send messages and media between each other in real time chats without relying on a centralized server. With enough adopters, WebTorrent may invert the economics of web hosting. Popular sites will be cheaper to host than less popular sites, without having to fall back on advertisement networks.

The web2web (https://github.com/elendirx/web2web) project uses Bitcoin and BitTorrent together to replace the entire web stack. The blockchain is searched for the last outgoing transaction from a given address. This transaction uses the OP_RETURN Bitcoin opcode to define the transaction as invalid, and stashes the torrent infohash in the transaction's body. This hash is enough to fetch the website being served through WebTorrent.

CacheP2P (http://www.cachep2p.com/) uses WebTorrent to offer a website cache. The reasoning is that popular content is likely to have a nearby peer which is closer than the nearest CDN server. CacheP2P, it's worth noting, costs the website maintainer nothing and costs each of the site's visitors a very small amount of traffic. This stands in contrast to the expensive caching infrastructure necessary to blanket a country or the globe. If a site becomes more popular in a certain area, CacheP2P will bring more cache servers to the region automatically. This latter point is a good enough argument alone.

RESOURCES

http://www.BitTorrent.org/beps/bep_0003.ht
ml

http://www.BitTorrent.org/beps/bep_0004.htm
l

http://www.BitTorrent.org/beps/bep_0005.htm
l

http://www.BitTorrent.org/beps/bep_0006.htm
l

http://www.BitTorrent.org/beps/bep_0009.htm
l

http://www.BitTorrent.org/beps/bep_0023.htm
l

http://www.BitTorrent.org/beps/bep_0027.htm
l

https://github.com/elendirx/web2web

https://webtorrent.io/

https://popcorntime.sh/en

Chapter 11

HOW OPENBAZAAR WORKS

Truly Free Trade Through Cryptography

INTRO

All of the privacy tools in the world won't help one if all of one's commerce is centralized through a few corporate websites that eagerly mine one's information to sell to advertisers and governments either directly or indirectly. With time, a person can be profiled and targeted. The classic example of the pressure-cooker-backpack police raid shows that United States online shopping has become a target of surveillance.

While most agree that customs and standardized import restrictions in the real world are useful, many dislike it online. One country may impose political views upon the entire rest of the world because of the location that a business incorporates. The ability to censor what is sold, to fix prices, and to impose localized trade restrictions degrades free trade. EBay, Amazon, and Etsy refuse to allow for resale of many items. This pushes users into the murky waters of sites without a verified trust system. Trust is the bedrock of online commerce.

OpenBazaar seeks to create a fully distributed marketplace protocol which optimizes for anonymity, freedom, trustworthiness, and convenience. The restriction of full distribution without any central arbitrators or global buyer enumeration forces a creative architecture that promises high scalability.

THREAT MODEL

OpenBazaar has two classes of enemies worth considering. The first wants to abuse the system much as users abuse existing commerce sites on a daily basis. The latter wants to perform an expensive, widespread attack to de-anonymize users or degrade the entire system.

Bad vendors and buyers are addressed very well through the power of multisig Bitcoin transactions and through OpenBazaar's web of trust model.

The web of trust (which we explain better later) allows a buyer who trusts a small number of peers to iteratively predict the trust they should place in another peer. This network is created through using external services, interaction, or personal history.

When a sale occurs, the buyer and vendor pick a peer that both trust and create a Bitcoin transaction which requires that two of the three parties agree to the transaction for it to be valid. This allows for arbitration without relying on a centralized support team. If one fears that a bad node may be picked, this type of contract can scale indefinitely. One could construct a system where eight of fifteen nodes must agree to the transaction. Shipping tracking information and terms of the sale are placed into a cryptographically-traceable ledger that acts as a log for arbitration.

Globally malicious attackers require a different type of strategy. Transactions occur over the blockchain, meaning that an impersonation (Sybil) attack would require an attacker to spend an unfeasible amount of money to overload vendors. In essence, they would simply be buying out the market and aiding business!

To impersonate a vendor, an attacker would need to gain trust by becoming a vendor. Once they begin acting badly and tying up arbitrator time, their reputation will suffer. In this way, a Sybil attack degrades into a failed attempt to game the system.

De-anonymization attacks are the only justified fear. OpenBazaar does a good job of tackling the problem better than previous solutions. By preventing one from seeing the entire web of trust, OpenBazaar prevents an adversary who can observe some mail and who know a few users' identities from inductively tracing down every purchaser and vendor.

A malicious vendor will be able to see one's IP address if Tor isn't used. Currently, Tor and OpenBazaar do not interoperate together perfectly. This is coming quite soon though, and current usage seems to be good enough for certain network operations. Oddly enough, OpenBazaar suggested one day rolling out an onion routing mail protocol. By encrypting subsequent addresses and sending the package to intermediate peers, one can mimic Tor and avoid exposing the sender address to the purchaser. This would carry a stamp cost, but may be able to keep people safe from persecution.

TECHNICAL DIFFICULTIES

Attackers are not the only challenge faced by OpenBazaar. OpenBazaar is prevented from making certain naive design choices due to their commitment to convenience and scalability.

While using a blockchain technology like Ethereum to host traffic would have been easy, it would have added an unacceptable latency and mining fee to each transaction. Furthermore, it's an expensive model for needless consistency. The network view is quite localized; a buyer only needs to talk to the vendor most of the time.

Reputation change is included in the Bitcoin blockchain, but this information is included in a Bitcoin transaction that would have to happen anyways.

Lastly, the commitment to full distribution forced OpenBazaar to make choices about what types of products they can create. OpenBazaar is primarily a protocol, not an application. There can be multiple frontends. This forced OpenBazaar to make a "machine readable" trade format that sends the required information over JSON. At the same time, "human readable" names must be used to allow users to familiarize themselves with vendors.

SALE ARCHITECTURE

The secret behind OpenBazaar's indefinite scalability is the use of their Kademlia-style distributed hash table. This DHT associates a globally unique identifier with a peer's hostname and port. This identifier is a self-signed public key that has been hashed twice. This GUID cannot be reused by another peer without access to the private key in the key pair.

Such a GUID would be unacceptably difficult to remember for most people; OpenBazaar can use the Blockstack system to associate identities with GUIDs. OpenBazaar initially used Namecoin, but switched to the alternative Blockstack. Blockstack embeds identities into any suitable blockchain, rather than requiring the separate Namecoin blockchain. This has the advantage of not requiring explicit support from mining pools, which increases the number of nodes mining the block. This, argues many, makes Blockstack more secure. Other information in the Blockstack entry can be used for external validation.

It's worth noting that external validation could compromise anonymity entirely for some vendors.

In order to allow for people to quickly find a peer's listed items, the DHT also contains the hashes and keywords for items that are listed for sale. After finding the hash of an item listing, a peer can then request this listing from the vendor in a direct P2P manner. If this architecture feels like BitTorrent, that is because it is remarkably similar.

These listings are known as Ricardian Contracts and are digitally signed documents with the necessary server information and public keys for a peer to resume the contract's back-and-forth. Contracts describe everything related to the listing, in a JSON-encoded document. The format is flexible enough that the merchant can describe the structure of payment and business that they expect from a buyer.

This means that OpenBazaar suits both digital and physical goods, and could potentially be used for labor and "sharing economy" tasks. Without a centralized authority taking a steep cut, OpenBazaar would be quite attractive. The web of trust that we will cover next can be used to establish a validated reputation to keep people safe.

WEB OF TRUST AND RATINGS

There are two cases that we trust a person in our daily lives. We typically either have had extensive interaction with a person, or we have had it with someone who trusts them very well. In OpenBazaar, this is also the case.

"Direct" trust can be established between people who validate each other's identity through other channels. If one doesn't have direct trust rating for a peer one wishes to query the evaluation of, one asks one's peers what their trust rating for the peer is. They perform a similar recursive check and query. Eventually, this bottoms out with a series of trust estimation chains.

A trust value ranges between 0 and 1 for positive trust, and 0 and -1 for distrust. The peers one will query from must be trusted, and must therefore have a trust between 0 and 1. This can therefore be used as a scale factor. By taking the product of the trusts along the chain, and summing up all such products, the query finds an aggregate trust for the peer for a node's corner of the web.

This system is entirely decentralized. The partial observability built into it also prevents de-anonymization through passive observation by a nation-state adversary. To avoid enumeration, nodes must only allow queries from trusted nodes.

There is one worrying attack that OpenBazaar is vulnerable to. A peer which copies the listings of another vendor could simply forward buyer requests to another peer. This would lead to an accumulation of trustworthy interactions with an untrustworthy individual. Furthermore, this attack is cheap. It could be done by almost anybody. The definitive way to check for one such abuse is for the vendor to include a copy of their GUID and key material inside the shipment. A buyer can therefore find out if something is wrong, and can spread news of distrust throughout the network. An adversary who is willing to receive and repackage shipments is essentially acting as a legitimate reseller.

This system can be insufficient though. The web of trust should be a single web; this system is not difficult to partition. In order to provide a global trust score for some users, an external resource must be burned to prevent someone from creating many globally-trusted accounts and bootstrapping evil peers of these accounts to be recommended indirectly. The current best solution to that is simply to buy your good graces. By using Bitcoin's scripting language to make coins unspendable while recording the user's hash, a user can provide global evidence that their account cost them money to keep. The economic disincentive for that peer to behave badly has been proven to the network.

The rating system is different. It's much more fine-grained for starters, enabling a review of shipment time and item quality as well as other attributes. Secondly, the goal is not to tell whether a peer is abusive but whether they offer a high-quality service. Ratings and reviews are documents in the DHT which have their hash embedded in the payment Bitcoin transaction. Ratings require transactions, which require a purchase with the vendor. Impersonation and Sybil attacks are mitigated in this way.

Vendors do not review buyers, as all opportunities for buyer abuse are mitigated or arbitrated away by the protocol.

SUCCESS OF PROTOCOL

There are currently between 5,000 and 5,500 listings posted to the OpenBazaar DHT. One can find everything from Alibaba purchases to expensive teas to physical and digital artwork. The network is slowly but steadily growing, and appears to have a lot of users who remain lightly active.

The myriad of implementations are likely the reason. The official desktop application is a JavaScript desktop application written using the Electron shell. For mobile, there is BazaarHound. Both of these allow for interactive exploration and make it easy to instantaneously purchase an order.

Search on the applications could be better though. For this, there are two popular search engines: DuoSear.ch and BazaarBay. The former appears much more polished, competing with many small-time centralized interfaces for quality.

The official desktop application can be made to work through Tor, to add and another layer of anonymity. Information about one's host may be leaked by the information in the protocol itself though, and it's not clear right now how much the software will expose. In OpenBazaar 2.0, CoinDesk promised Tor integration from the ground up. The reliance on the IPFS (inter-planetary filesystem, a BitTorrent-like file network) means that IPFS must work perfectly with Tor for OpenBazaar to.

This protocol has multiple implementations and is growing to carry many goods at great prices. The flexibility and trustworthiness of the service means that OpenBazaar makes an amazing privacy-enhancing platform upon which to build new e-commerce applications.

REFERENCES

http://docs.openbazaar.org/

http://www.bazaarhound.com/

https://github.com/OpenBazaar/openbazaar-go/issues/99

http://bazaarbay.org/

https://duosear.ch/

http://www.nydailynews.com/news/national/lo
ng-island-woman-claims-online-search-pressure-
cooker-helped-prompt-visit-feds-article-1.1415101

https://blockstack.org/papers

https://blockstack.org/docs/blockstack-vs-
namecoin

Chapter 12

TRUSTLESS DESIGN PATTERNS

Doing It Yourself

INTRO

It's time for a new project. Rather than throwing up an MVC web framework and a SQL server, let's design this as a P2P system without any centralization. Before reaching for the most hyped buzzword, it's important to understand exactly what problems you have. In all likelihood, your system is not a special snowflake. People have had similar problems before and have solved them in a myriad of ways. These ideas have stood the test of time; attackers have attempted to exploit them for profit at every turn. The systems which have stuck around have done so because they're doing something right.

I will attempt to provide a domain analysis for distributed, trustless, peer-to-peer architectures. I will walk the reader through the questions that should be asked, and how each will impact the inevitable design.

DOMAIN MODELING METHODOLOGY

Part of the difficulty of designing trustless distributed systems is in deciding what it is that needs to be distributed. The usage prescribes the architecture much more than in traditional MVC applications, but design patterns have begun to emerge. Below, I will walk one through taking a rough idea and generating a system architecture to refine. Later, I will walk the reader through doing so with a new project.

Step 0: Identify Provided Services

Every great project starts as an idea. If the reader doesn't have an idea for what they want to make, I suggest considering the problems of the world. Make something useful. Consider how much of modern society is coordination of information between people. There is the market price of a good, the news, debts, speculation on corporation valuations, social networking, donation, education (testing!), elections, privacy, and entertainment. Find something you care about, and consider what modeling it could achieve when used pervasively.

Now stop and write out the roles of the people you expect to be getting services from your system and providing services to your system. You're going to need to be very comfortable with these, as permission changes will ripple throughout the remaining steps.

Ask yourself if you're going to prioritize anonymity of user actions at the account level or at the network level. Anonymizing at the network level can be accomplished by sending around a Tor address rather than the client's IP address, and by not overwhelming the network with traffic. Anonymizing at the account level is more difficult, but is a lot more useful. ZeroCash is an example, as is Tor itself. Tor uses partial observability through onion routing to hide portions of a user's actions from other peers. ZeroCash, on the other hand, uses zero-knowledge proof to cryptographically mix resources.

Step 1: Identify the Shared Data Structures

Modeling is a field of study outside the scope of this entry. Note that following foreign keys requires another query typically. As following a pointer in a native object may cause a cache miss, so too may a hash in a node of a distributed data structure. Optimization here is the same as for cache-aware, thread-safe data structures. If immutable, one can embed objects into their referrers and trade space for latency.

Most of the time, one just needs a row and column database that has a primary key and queryable attributes. In a P2P system, this primary key is "owned" by those who can write to it.

Some questions around the importance of history arise. If the current world of the system is dependent upon a globally-known history, one might wish to reach for a distributed ledger. If other keys need to have certain values in order for a write to be allowed, one should place this transition into a blockchain. The easiest way to determine if one should use a blockchain is to ask yourself if you would need to take a lock for this field if this program was local and multithreaded. If the field belongs only to one writer, then no. Else, you'd better use locks to prevent race conditions. Locks can be modeled with transactions, and distributed transaction ledgers are most commonly served by blockchain nowadays.

One of the easier ways to decompose a program into transactions is to look at the state machines hidden in your program and to explicitly model them.

Note that blockchains, like locks, impose a serial nature to computation that results in a dramatic performance loss. There are special conditions that allow for faster micro-transactions at times, but these are difficult to exploit.

Ask yourself what form a user should take in the system. Are they a session or a person? Do they need to be identified by a unique address? What kind of encryption makes sense when communicating with them? Do they have a long-lived trust score, or are they ephemeral? Where is their identity stored? Is it available offline? Something that is important to grasp is that everything that is done needs to be provably from someone. A system cannot rely on the network address to be a good unique address for the peer. A peer needs a secret that proves identity, and they need to link this secret to their unique address in the network. A public/private key pair is a good one. Previously, the key material was too large to appear in the distributed addresses. Modern elliptic-curve cryptography allows for much smaller public keys. Many systems still use hashes of the public keys.

Lastly, ask yourself if you're working as a courier of communication between two other parties or if you are providing content yourself. In either, you should figure out how you explicitly want to model each type of communication in the protocol. The packets are data structures too; consider how they should be laid out.

Step 2: Identify Data Structure Update Permissions

Now for each data structure, keep breaking it down until you can say definitively who owns each object. If an object has keys that have different permissions, partition the object into object fragments. Decide how you want to encode the people who can access the fragment.

If there is ever an object fragment owned by multiple people, ask yourself who owns it when. If the permissions can be cleanly separated, consider if you can chain their messages by placing the hash of a previous message in the reply. The logic for permissions can be embedded in blocks, passing off permission temporarily. The chain of messages can themselves be stored in the data structure. Therefore there is an explicit ordering and bad transactions can be dropped. Nodes that reject bad transactions can keep appending by referring to the last good transaction in their predecessor hash field.

Now ask yourself if there need to be explicit correctness checks before saving fields for this fragment. If the object fragment needs it, you need a blockchain. You might be able to get away with multiple, small blockchains if the number of keys are If so, ask yourself the lifecycle of updates. If the permission to write will move between people explicitly, then you can encode the transfer in an existing blockchain. Refer to the data element by the hash of the transaction that "begins" the history of the field. Now send a transaction from this account with embedded data to the blockchain address of the recipient of the key. In this way, the key is sent like currency.

If you're lucky and don't need a blockchain, then you can use a DHT. The key of a piece of data must have the public key of the data's owner associated with it, or the hash of the data. It is a public key if we want the DHT to be able to verify that updates pushed to a key are signed by the public key of the owner. We want a hash if we want to use the DHT for content storage. While external tracking (blockchains, Namecoin) is an option, it brings risks and scalability bottlenecks with it. A web of trust is a nice solution but requires that one trust a few people in the network. This puts those strangers joining the network at some risk. Having the key into the DHT contain the hash of the data, the hash of the data signer, or the hash of the transaction with a history of the ownership, allows one to place trust only in crypto.

Step 3: Identify Data Structure Visibility and Persistence

Stop and write out your use cases for your application. For each of them list the following:

1. The input you expect to receive from the service-consumer

2. The output that you expect to receive from the system

   1. Any messages you expect to happen in-between.

Now ask yourself which of these steps changes or reads from a shared a data structure, and how.

Now consider how to rate-limit reads and writes from the shared data structure. Proof-of-work is a popular solution. Few others take the burden of rate limiting off of the peers providing services to such a degree. Also, ask yourself if there is a way to limit read permissions to those who need it. To protect both privacy and performance, build as ungenerous a system as you can get away with.

Now ask yourself how long the data from a write is going to remain in the global data structures and how much of it a peer needs to see to provide or request services. "Forever" and "all of it" is not an acceptable answer most of the time. Blockchains require the ability to summarize themselves so that most nodes don't need the entire chain. A DHT key will time out eventually if peers don't interact with it. A distributed system must garbage collect, or it will overflow.

With the costs of data retention in mind, ask yourself who is going to be responsible for keeping the data necessary to provide the system's promises. If the system requires data to be kept for verification, ask yourself if the consistency structures and the content structures can be divorced. By placing hashes for data in the consistency structures, they can be kept small. Once one need only to provide key-value access without consistency, it is possible to use a DHT or something like BitTorrent to distribute the file chunks.

A file hash removes the need to trust content distributors.

Ask yourself who needs to know when a data structure changes on a case-by-case basis. Decide whether each individual case should be "push" or "pull". In a "push" system, the peer gets updates sent to them by another peer in the cluster. Alternatively, asynchronous messaging or email can be used. In a "pull" system, the data structure is simply updated and the peers must check keys for changes.

Lastly, ask yourself if a user needs to be able to get messages while offline. If not, is enough key information online to communicate with the peer? A public key is sufficient but is unsuitable for systems promising perfect forward secrecy. Here, one should turn to negotiation of temporary symmetric keys. If asynchronous or "push" notification is being used, one might need prekeys (see Signal). Pre-keys can be used for non-interactive symmetric key negotiation.

Step 4: Identify Legal State Transitions

Now, document the state transitions that are legal and document them in the encoding that the previous sections motivated you to arrive upon. Consider when they will occur. Consider planned latency, asynchronous messages, and transactions. Nothing can help clarify a system with innumerable boxes and arrows as much as actually going through the state machines and data structure operations.

Step 5: Identify The Nature of Each Identity

Below, we will draw distinctions between service consumers and service providers. While a peer in a distributed system tends to be both, this is not always the case. Here, we describe them separately. A system can trivially present them together instead.

Now that you've figured out the steps that users can take and who can take them, it's time to consider the face that service consumers will show to the system. We must be aware that if we make it too easy to become a new user, someone may pretend to be many people. This can be used to unbalance voting power and to steal resources from the system.

For many systems, like Tor, the service consumer doesn't have a long-lasting identity. The service provider does, in order to be contacted and to build a trust profile. The service consumer is known by a provider for the duration of the time that the provider is servicing the consumer. This model offers maximal privacy but means that the system cannot use a consumer's identity to prevent abuse of service. Rate limiting in this model must be done on each endpoint request.

For longer-lasting identities, the system must find a way to associate information with the user. The user's interaction with service providers should be cryptographically signed to prevent peers from lying about each other.

Here we see two options. The first is that we have a distributed consensus around a document. Peers are chosen at random to validate the document's contents. The size of the network and a rate limit on measurement works to buffer against a rush by bad actors. The second option is to have a web of trust and to rely on the carefulness of peers trusted from external connections or from experience. The latter is much more resilient in small networks but is vulnerable to partitions. If a peer in a web can only see evil agents, they will have a bad time.

Step 6: Identify Sharing and Linking

This brings us to one of the most important questions to ask about a new system. How will users link into the system? The service-providing peers need to receive a request somehow. It's important to note that most systems have no means to provide a practical "search." For some, the work would be immense and poll-heavy. In order to interoperate with other systems, your system needs an equivalent of a hyperlink. Someone must be able to connect and fetch content with no interaction beyond presenting this string.

This necessity is reflected in all successful systems. For Tor, it's a hidden address. For BitTorrent, it is a peer IP and the torrent InfoHash. For Bitcoin, it's an address. Most systems don't go far enough, and have a plethora of independent websites to index them. Stop and ask yourself if a DNS-like system would make more sense. Do you want someone to be able to use an easy-to-remember string to fetch a resource? Namecoin and Blockstack are two systems that can impose a mapping of a short name to a number of addresses on diverse services.

Now ask yourself how you trust that a BitTorrent file is not a virus. It's because of the context associated with how you got the torrent metadata. The tracker or indexer of the hash will have some reputation. People who download will be commenting and vetting it. What will your site have? There will be bad users not performing a Sybil attack. They will need some way to weed them out. How do you prevent this from being abused? How do you keep people honest? I suggest you provide some way for peers use cryptographically-signed evidence to prove wrongdoing, and build conflict resolution into the protocol.

Step 7: Identify Peer Evaluation and Reward

Now ask yourself how to tell how well a peer is providing services to other peers. For Bitcoin, the peers who mine with the most power over a given time period are most likely to win the transaction fee. For many other systems, it's more feasible to reward people on a finer grain.

Most systems will embed the peer's identity into the data structure transition they are overseeing in some way. In Bitcoin, for instance, the payout goes to the miner. When storing evidence of a transaction, include the server in order to give something to reward. If privacy concerns make this unacceptable, turn to distributed measuring and gossip.

Have peers record the latency of connections with each other and communicate with the data structure tracking measurements. Since identities have some cost, this will ensure that as long as a majority of users are honest, the measurements should be honest. Because the documents are signed by peers, it doesn't matter who presents them to other peers. Signing a message allows it to be redistributed as evidence. This is known as non-repudiation. This lax data-origin constraint means that a DHT works well here for storage.

Something that is an uneasy option is centralization here. By having a vetting group to measure servers secretly, one can ensure that the network's quality-of-service information is correct. Incorrect documents could lead to a minor DOS. This becomes a point of failure for the system. On the other hand, we have seen that this type of system can work. It provides optimistically assured security to a critical regulation function.

A web of trust could work here but would have to be securely bootstrapped externally.

Step 8: Choose a Cost for Identity Creation and Service Consumption

A P2P system shares resources. If there were no bookkeeping done to prevent overuse of resources, a tragedy of the commons would result. One must ensure that the rate of consuming resources has some cost to the consumer. It would be nice if this cost contributes to the functioning of the system, but can serve only rate limiting if need be. In a P2P distributed system, the most precious resource is an orderly, correct data structure. Changes require the synchronization of peers, which takes bandwidth. This is why one must turn to rate limiting to protect the shared data of the system.

Most DHTs have a few recovery mechanisms. The first is that the key contains a hash of the value, which makes it very difficult to forge a response. This means that the only real fear is that one will insert a lot of junk data. We defeat this fear with a short expiration time and the ability to turn to proof-of-work rate limiting on insertion.

Guarding blockchains is done through mining by expending external assets. Proof-of-work requires guessing in a way that requires computational power. Proof-of-stake forces one to leave currency unused for a long period of time. This imposes an external cost on doing the work that is rewarded.

Guarding identity is another important thing to do. Implicit in many architectures is the idea that involving multiple peers makes something more trustworthy. If it is cheap for someone to register themselves as multiple peers, the effectiveness of this process goes down significantly. Proof-of-work is one way to rate limit identity creation. It can be so computationally wasteful; one may wish instead to have a peer perform useful work that can be measured and vetted in order to earn the right to consume system resources.

At the end of the day, the cost should be externalized. It can be time, computation, currency, bandwidth, or something else. It must be something that has a cost which scales with increased usage. It must be something that makes it too expensive to attack the system.

SOLUTIONS AND STRATEGIES

Distributed Data Structures

Purely Functional / Hashed

Good distributed data structures are good purely functional data structures. Any time that the updates to a system must be tracked individually, the data structure becomes more or less immutable. Having a single-reference compare-and-set allows one to serialize transactions trivially.

To take a purely functional data structure and yield a good distributed data structure, replace pointers to either embedded copies of the data, or hashes of the data. Hashes are immutable, meaning that circular references or loops are not possible in these structures. A complex operation can be done by chaining updates and by keeping succinct representations cached. Merkle trees and Patricia trees are examples of the method that these structures can offer proofs of membership very cheaply.

Hashes can offer that level of indirection which solves many of the hard problems in computer science.

Mutable

Standing in direct opposition to this idea is the common practice of embedding objects in a DHT. A DHT is much like RAM. A key (pointer) refers to content. One can generate an address somehow, and use it to store arbitrary data. A circular reference is trivial in a DHT, as the addresses are not content hashes but key hashes. One of the nice things about using a DHT is that it is garbage-collecting. If a peer drops in and out of the network (such as on a cellular connection) then the data will remain in the DHT for a short while. When the peer has remained offline for long enough, it will expire and be purged.

Decoupled Control

One of the easier changes to make is to decouple control structures from data storage structures. By storing the data structures that describe the shape of the data externally, it is possible to manipulate it without having to fetch the data. For large data structures, this can be very useful.

An example of this would be the metadata of a torrent and the peer list that a tracker distributes. A peer can get a view of the data structure's block availability in the cluster without having to skip around large data files. This also allows torrents to be "streamed" by downloading blocks sequentially and allowing one to skip to an offset in the file.

Another example is the way that Bitcoin blocks indirect the contained transactions. A hash of the root of a Merkle tree is stored rather than the transactions in the block. The ability to check whether a transaction is in the blockchain without storing the entire blockchain increases the number of peers who can interact with the blockchain in a useful way.

Peer Discovery

Peer discovery is the problem of distributing copies of the information associated with a peer. More than just the problem of consistency, key distribution is classically a hard problem in encryption. That peer discovery is a nontrivial problem is proven by a long history of failures.

The first question to ask is whether you can afford for this part of the system to be distributed. The second question is to ask if you can afford it not to be. A centralized peering system is harder to run a Sybil attack against, but each trusted peer has a bullseye on themselves. Someone need only compromise this handful of machines to compromise the system. A centralized peering system is thus architecturally more simple but builds in an Achilles heel.

A centralized peering protocol would be carried out by having service-providing peers send a small group of trusted peers their documents. The peers should use a trusted-peer consensus algorithm such as Raft or Paxos to agree on a list of peers to sign and distribute. Note that if your system features distributed measuring of peers (recommended) then the measurements will probably go to these servers as well. These centralized systems are the Tor directory servers, the Signal servers, and the BitTorrent trackers of the world. Note that by storing very little information on the peers, one may reduce the usefulness of compromise to a negligible amount. Signal has done this well.

Distributed peering system are attractive, but perfection is intractable. Brewer's Theorem, also known as the CAP theorem, tells us that a distributed system can provide only two of the three goals of prompt consistency, availability, or partition-tolerance. Consistency refers to whether the peers in the system will all see the same state transitions of the system. Eventual consistency, a weaker goal, says that peers will all arrive at the same state in a bounded amount of time. Note that these properties can be used to study a system as a whole, or a part of a system in isolation.

Which two do you want to pick for the isolated peering system? Partition-tolerance, if sacrificed, means that losing messages will result in the system going down. This is clearly a non-starter. Now if you sacrifice consistency entirely then a peer can split your distributed system into smaller and smaller pieces until each can be overwhelmed by coordinated attacks from a wealthy attacker. If you sacrifice availability, then some of the requests may never get a response. Not even Bitcoin escapes this principle. (http://paulkernfeld.com/2016/01/15/Bitcoin-cap-theorem.html)

The most straightforward way to do distributed registration is a DHT (hopefully with rate limiting). A DHT works by ensuring that the routers have enough of a connection such that no nodes are entirely outside of the network. If a network partition does occur and segregates all nodes which hold the content behind a given key, then the system simply loses the data. If a peer recognizes that their key is lost, they can re-insert. Given some kind of count of the number of updates at a key, when nodes re-join the cluster they can figure out how to rejoin the network following some pre-defined collision scheme. We see that DHTs are not perfect solutions, but are acceptable in many cases.

Either way, both systems must consider a few things. First of all, consider how the document will be distributed in a scalable manner. If you're passing around the file in a P2P manner, ask yourself how the hashes and the signature public keys should be distributed. A peer's "state" document signed with the peer's private key is only secured if the public key distribution method is trustworthy.

Furthermore, one must protect against a replay attack. An attacker who wishes to keep the size of the network small can re-distribute previous documents if there is no safeguard. Peers receiving the replayed document will get a view of the network which will motivate them to behave in a way that disrupts the network. An example of a possible attack is to send around a list which is out of date for all but one peer. This remaining online peer will get all of your online traffic. In this way, an adversary could intelligently replay documents to certain peers to coordinate a distributed stress attack on a peer.

Documents thus require a timestamp and expiration policy. Note that a vector clock timestamp or blockchain is not enough, as timestamps must be able to generate an expiration time. Without an expiration time, an evil peer could replay a single older state indefinitely to new peers joining the network. These peers would not have a way to tell how long ago the document was released.

Peer Work Allocation

Now that you've chosen your trustless and distributed data store for peer discovery, you must decide how to use it. How will peers be chosen to service a request? This is more than just an implementation detail. Tor's privacy comes in large part because the only person to pick the next peer in the chain is the client having their data routed. Having consumers pick peers to interact with tends to have better security than having some coordinated peer distribution algorithm.

One is advised to perform a random shuffle on the peer list and to build in load average feedback and work refusal to avoid running into pathological bad cases. Indeed, one should consider how to try to ensure that the load is optimally balanced across the cluster. Done wrong and your entire distributed system might saturate a few nodes which are alphabetically first.

Peer Reward

Ask yourself what rewards peers get for participating in the system and what it costs to become a service-providing peer. It's important that no peer can get more from misusing the system than an attack must cost them.

If it's free to become a peer, then you will suffer from Sybil attacks. Costs don't always have to be proof-of-work. BitTorrent has a peer pay its "cost" when it has seeded enough to be unchoked by a peer and to be trusted by the tracker. Tor costs are bandwidth over time. Consistent bandwidth allocation to Tor makes a peer trusted.

Proof-of-work has become a quite easy reusable cost, but note that it is entirely useless work. Unlike the mentioned measured contributions, proof-of-work work serves only to solve a hashing puzzle.

Distributed Content Querying

Something worth considering is that many people will simply not use your system if information takes more than a few seconds to search. This prohibits requiring peer connections during the search. If one is rate limiting fetching values from the DHT, this means that an index (like a database index) is probably necessary.

The real moral here is that you most likely won't get queries "for free" unless you build them in from the beginning. Carefully ask yourself how to amortize search by building up a structure at insertion time that's easy for a client to access offline or with a connection to a single peer or handful of peers.

Asynchronous Sessions

Let's consider a more modern concern related to distributed systems. In most older systems, a peer that has been down for a few hours is dead to the network. In a modern system, it is important to allow for service consumers to connect and disconnect without immediately being blacklisted.

It's worth noting that the issues of the architecture reflect the issues of the underlying protocol. A P2P socket stream between peers is notoriously difficult to maintain on modern networks.

On the other hand, encrypted information can easily be channeled over other mediums. It's worth noting that the rate limits applied inside the system may not extend to external systems. Giving out a user's phone number without some kind of severe rate limiting or brute-force-discovery throttling is irresponsible.

The requirement to keep pending messages or key material puts a burden of storage on the network. If one wants to incorporate this, they must ask how the service will be provided and who will be rewarded for providing it.

A sane middle ground is to use a DHT with a timeout to act as a cache for user details. Another option is to embed information in a blockchain. Unfortunately, both options typically require an additional system to rate limit and to handle revocations or key material destruction after exposure.

Privacy

Privacy is the ultimate requirement to consider in a distributed system. Every degree that a service consumer or service provider privacy is not protected is another degree that the system can be attacked. If peer discovery is not made difficult enough, a nation-state can trivially blacklist all entry points. In oppressive countries, people might have their lives threatened by lax privacy guarantees. What can be done?

The first thing is to ask yourself if you're storing more information than is necessary, or more precise information than is necessary. Does a millisecond accurate timestamp really need to be used to store evidence of something? Do any logs really need to be stored? Could someone look at the network and find the IP address of a person to interrogate for access to the information? Is there any peer who acts as a single-point-of-identification, such that sending a packet to them results in culpability? If so, your system isn't secure.

Secondly, ask yourself if you have unencrypted data being sent between peers at any point in the network. There is never any reason to require that. Many people assume the cost of a secure connection is much higher than it is. In reality, connections between peers should be long-lived enough that encryption costs are a minuscule fraction of the total stream bandwidth. Key negotiation is easier nowadays than most know. Not only can two online hosts perform interactive key negotiation that is resilient against attackers, the advent of prekeys means that one can upload pre-computed halves of the negotiation to allow for asynchronous/bulked encryption without the network latency of a round-trip.

Furthermore, successful encryption means that the socket of the data does not need to be unbroken for security to be assured. By updating keys with each message in a double-ratchet, one can be assured that key material stored on devices cannot be used to decrypt traffic recorded in the past. This enables true history erasure once each party has erased local logs.

For systems which have high privacy concerns, onion routing should be considered as an option. Messages can be pre-encrypted and passed along to nodes to be forwarded to the final destination. This doesn't need to be a heavyweight Tor-scale setup; this principle can be used to prevent insertion tracking on DHTs and other distributed data structures.

If it's not worth the effort to build support in anonymity yourself, please do not make it harder for people to use Tor with your system. Concerns should be noted with respect to sending automatically-fetched IP addresses over Tor, which defeats the purpose of the network. Allow manual hidden service ID insertion instead. Likewise, DNS policy should be audited for potential leaks.

Lastly, consider encrypting any balances of network resources. An intelligent attacker might be able to use the rate of changes to associate an identity with a server. Instead, prefer a system using zero-knowledge proofs to track proxies of value. ZeroCash is a great example here.

PRESENTATION AND MINIMUMS

The documentation of your system is significantly more important than the first release of your software. This is something that is difficult for many to grasp. Your system should be thought of as a protocol, not as "what my app does."

Your system is successful if and only if there are many independent implementations of the software.

Your system is successful if and only if the documentation is accessible enough for anybody to verify that an implementation meets the specification.

Your system is successful if and only if other systems can link into your system with ease.

Your system is successful if and only if peers are willing to pay the associated costs because they trust the system to fulfill their request.

Your system is successful if and only if your documentation is good enough that implementers trust their understanding of it.

Presentation Conventions

We see now that the protocol presentation is important. The current style is to have a "white paper," a formatted article with a number of subsections chosen by convention.

You may choose alternative presentations, but it is important that you answer some questions in your first release. You should explicitly enumerate the attacks that someone may try to make on your system, and how you defend against each. You should make a mention to previous works in the same vein, in order to put your contributions in context.

Audits

Expect for some of your assertions to be wrong. Expect to find a reader who is an expert in some sub-field and has noticed a terrible mistake in your system. If you're lucky, they'll come forward before you launch and offer them an economic incentive to attack it.

Reward your auditors if you can, and always try to find experts who can confirm or deny the economic and security assertions you make in your system.

Upgrade Compatibility

With the knowledge that software in general is terrible, planning for the future is paramount. In software, that means planning for protocol upgrades.

Each message should contain the version of the protocol that the peer is operating on. This allows for peers to figure out how to interpret messages from out-of-date peers and who to intelligently refuse to interact with. Furthermore, try to build in an extension protocol for others to piggyback extra information on. This allows for peers with certain clients to use an upgraded protocol without breaking compatibility with the rest of the network.

Launch

Now that the fun part is over, prepare to defend your architecture for the rest of time. You've probably made some mistakes that the first few auditors haven't caught. It's important to put yourself out there and to fail in a way that doesn't hurt anybody. Because of this, it's recommended to host a test network for anybody interested in the technology to experiment with. Log enough to explain failures.

Learn from your mistakes, publicly warn the world while they are vulnerable, and patch quickly without releasing new bugs. Above all, retain the trust of your community.

If you lose the trust of your community, you lose the ability to easily profit from your technology. At worst, you'll lose all of your peers. If you designed your system fairly, peers will be able to exclude you from it if you lose their trust.

RESOURCES

Bitcoin and CAP:

http://paulkernfeld.com/2016/01/15/Bitcoin-cap-theorem.html

Chapter 13

DESIGN WALK-THROUGH

INTRO

Examples can make all of the difference in comprehension. This chapter is an example usage of our framework. This is a high-level design walk-through; more exact details of the system are found in Appendix A.

MOTIVATION

"Absolute power corrupts absolutely" is a saying that is often used as justification for the madness of kings. The costs of maintaining control push one to reason that one has a duty to extract every last bit of profitability or utility off of it. Rather than growing the kingdom and profiting from the established means of reward, a king may choose the local minima of exploiting those who give him power in order to have a secure reward. Modern systems put absolute power in the hands of the person who owns a website. This is in large part because it becomes necessary for the author of the website to provide computer hosting for the website. This is both a blessing and a curse.

With power comes the ability to find novel ways to profit from the system in ways outside of the site's social contract. Even if the system only needs to save a few bits of information about each user to provide service, the system may need to see much more about the user in order to create the inserted data or to create an interface for the user. The user has no idea how much of their data is saved. If they consent to be tracked, the contract tends to be a single opt-in which gives a blanket pardon for collecting all of this data.

On the negative side, power comes with the ability to harm without retribution. Through misrepresentation or denial of service, the server can decide which users should be ostracized. Major social networks are accused of selectively displaying certain kinds of information in order to engineer a worldview in their users. Users point at the identity representation that the application has and says "this is me," while having no final say on what that representation holds. This is much like a King's authority to edit the society's stories to be more flattering.

All of this power comes at a cost. On the internet, you may be a king, but someone with a warrant can compel you to use this power in their interests. The more popular your service becomes, the more likely it is that attackers will find any vulnerability you have. The legacy of kings is one of anxiety and bloodshed for a reason; nature abhors a power vacuum.

GOLEM: TRUSTLESS, STATEFUL P2P

APPLICATION BACKENDS

The problem of power centralization is caused by placing the duty of data storage and manipulation in the hands of the maintainer-owned server. The Internet at large has been trying to fix this through peer-to-peer systems since the days of Napster. We've never quite gotten it right, though.

The core issue is one of abuse and data integrity. If anybody can control your database, it becomes impossible to ensure that a bad actor doesn't remove all of your records and destroy your system. An easy answer is to use encryption to make sure that an updater "owns" the data to be inserted. This works for messaging and file-sharing systems. This is not sufficient in most systems because the data will typically hold semantics that constrains the values. It is the application code's sequencing of updates that constrains data transitions.

If the data-manipulating application code is allowed to run on the client machines, it becomes increasingly difficult to ensure that the requests made by the client are requests that are formed by the application. Furthermore, clients have a copy of the code to reverse-engineer and copy. This is the real motivation behind client-server web apps. They're not a perfect solution though. If data-manipulating application code is run by the maintainer of the website, then they are in a position to be forced to eavesdrop or manipulate it.

What if somebody else ran the code responsible for validating and altering the database? It's not intuitive why this would improve anything. This person would see the client's intermediate sensitive data, could use it to generate an invalid data alteration, can reverse-engineer the code, and has less investment in software correctness than a good user and a good maintainer.

The Golem project arose from a desire to counteract each of these problems through knowledge limitation, intimate accounting of state changes, pervasive rate limiting, and cryptographically-validated identities.

PROCESS

Step 0: Identify Provided Services

So the end goal is for the system to perform the tasks of a traditional web application. In response to input from the service consumer, the code will be executed to determine which database transactions to run and how to render the result from the shared data.

For the sake of clarity, we will start by considering the people interacting with the system. There's the consumer (the website visitor), the supervisor (the code author and system runner), and the server (the code executor).

Now the supervisor needs a way to distribute their code in a way that protects it from trivial reverse engineering. The server needs to be able to get the code and run it in response to messages from consumers.

The idea here is to protect the consumer's information in the chance that the supervisor is compromised. We want it such that the consumer gets to see what is inserted in the database and that no party other than the consumer sees enough of the computation to compromise the information sent to the endpoints. I intend to use the idea of onion routing to have each server run a tiny fragment of the total application and then pass the encrypted remaining parameters onto a different server that can decrypt a few of them and perform a small step as well.

Step 1: Identify the Shared Data Structures

In an MVC web application, the shared database is the singular shared data structure. We have a collection of application servers that can modify any part of the shared data. When they read from it, they tend to use an index to make lightning-quick queries in a time less than O(N).

We need a way to create a trusted index of the system, and for people to modify the backing data store. Cache invalidation is one of the two hard problems in Computer Science (naming things being the other one). We will need to consider it in our design.

Step 2: Identify Data Structure Update Permissions

Let's dissect our monolithic database and see what each actor needs to be able to do with it.

A knee-jerk response is to say that customers shouldn't do anything themselves and that only servers need to read data and write data. Do they really, though? If a server is to be quasi-untrusted, then why should we trust writing to them? A server could allow another actor to do the data manipulation, a trusted actor. But what do we trust an actor with?

Let's only trust the customers to do updates and deletes. That makes it easy to say who owns the data; the people that the data pertains to owns it. This takes on the view of the database as a series of rows or documents, each owned by one or more customers. For now, let's limit each row to one customer. An explicit policy with regard to pre-published groups of keys rather than individual keys is just a matter of configuration here.

What about the indexes? Now an index really could be used for multiple things. If the index is how a consumer checks for the version of another consumer's row to use, then it's both a cache and a kind of verification. If we ask ourselves which users are the ones that are trusted to sign off on the state of the system, we see that the supervisor fits here.

Step 3: Identify Data Structure Visibility and Persistence

Now the shared global data store should be visible to everybody because we don't really have a good method of gating visibility beyond the encryption that users can negotiate end-to-end on their own. A global policy wouldn't make sense.

Furthermore, if the consumer is doing the updates then they get to proofread what's being inserted. They can choose to not insert entire transactions (but not individual updates) if a transaction contains compromising information.

Now, let's consider update subscriptions. The new version of the data needs to be tracked somewhere that the supervisor can verify and include in the updates of the index structures. Furthermore, we need some history to make it possible for a peer to manually validate the transaction history at a given key. This makes us reach for a blockchain.

If we're using a blockchain, we don't want to embed the actual data. What we can do here is post the reference to the new data in a transaction on the blockchain. The minuscule transaction fees here work as a rate limit to prevent denial of service attacks against the structure. This hash can be the torrent containing the information needed to construct a view of the data. Each index should also be a published as a torrent hash. The index structure's primary keys for the rows will be torrent hashes.

This decouples the data structure from the carried content and enables complex rate limiting and data retention policies. A supervisor who cares about data longevity can seed the torrents provided by the peers. A supervisor who wants ephemerality can allow peers to seed their own database keys, taking responsibility for the uptime of their data.

Step 4: Identify Legal State Transitions

In an MVC application, the servers are trusted to modify data in the database because the servers have a known codebase. They will perform explicit or implicit transactions that group updates together to form state machine transitions and update data that meets content validation.

In our system, we must ensure that an insertion will only follow a specific set of transactions. One way we can do this is to have the supervisor exploit the difficulty of prime factorization. Assign the code for each server a unique prime per query. Now a consumer connecting to the network will pick a random "accumulator" number to associate with the transaction. Each server in the process will append the query onto a transaction list to execute, and will multiply the accumulator by the prime stamp and will sign the transaction document.

Now a client who agrees to insert the transactions can insert the hash of this document at every key updated. Upon seeing one document, a supervisor will look at all other keys and will propagate the update if it is missing. It will also check that each server signed a transaction with one of the primes allocated to them at the end of the linked list. It can publish the list of acceptable prime products that make up valid transactions later. Any peer can then check that each transaction is divisible by one of the primes for the time slice.

Step 5: Identify the Nature of Each Identity

Since servers are trusted with code and consumers are trusted with keys, we cannot avoid needing to consider explicit identities in the system.

Now a consumer's identity is composite. Each request to the network is an identity of sorts. Without a global rate limiting state to track the number of live requests, the best way to prevent a rate limit is to require proof-of-work on each request. This we will do.

A consumer's database identity is longer-lived and consists of a key pair associated with the database keys the consumer can manipulate. A consumer doesn't need to be online or able to get incoming messages, so no IP is added.

A server's identity is necessary for them to get the code from the supervisor, and for them to get paid for serving the application. Therefore, we use proof-of-work to add a cost to joining. A server's identity includes their network addresses.

A supervisor's identity is their power. They control how the other two parties interact through their keys. All entities need to be able to get the public key of the supervisor. The supervisor does not need to be online. The files may be distributed by peers as long as hashes are trustworthy.

Step 6: Identify Sharing And Linking

We leave this problem to the users in part. There is a document published by the supervisor which shows the mapping of endpoints to servers which handle them. Linking the application involves linking access to a recent copy of this document.

Mapping endpoints to servers typically happens inside the server farm, requiring load-balancing infrastructure. Instead, we will take the Tor approach and enable customers to pick the servers they want to handle their request. Randomization is important here.

Step 7: Identify Peer Evaluation And Reward

The history of transactions should be able to be used by servers to show proof that they did work. The fact that a client can reject inserting a transaction means that the update should probably leave a signed "receipt" with the server in order to make that bookkeeping useful. We will limit the bandwidth reward to a capped amount per consumer per time-slice to prevent collusion and Sybil attacks. We have a middle-ground, where server receipts include the hashes of database transactions that include their keys. This, the ability to search out client keys, and the proof-of-work on all identity creation works against trying to exploit this.

We will reward servers with a microtransaction. The system will have explicit time-steps, and servers will be able to get a fine-grained payout to allow signing off before a time-step ends.

Step 8: Choose a cost for Identity Creation and Service Consumption

Now we will provide a number of types of costs. First, everybody does proof-of-work on everything which takes cluster resources. Most of the time, the difficulty is low enough that it shouldn't discourage anybody. Furthermore, we will require that servers pay the supervisor a tiny fragment at the start of each tick period. The supervisor pays this fee back at the start of the microtransaction, locking the coins in an inaccessible limbo until the time period is over. This externalizes the cost of participation, to make denial of service attacks expensive.

Here we see that it's desirable to provide means for the supervisor to directly profit from site interaction as well. Otherwise, there is no monetary incentive to run the site. The receipts that servers have and the transactions that customers insert can all be forced to contain hashes of "tokens" that can be purchased from the supervisor. Tokens might be literal magic values, or they might be the hashes of microtransaction blocks that have been made between the customer and supervisor.

At the end of the day, the "token" is used to incentivize the supervisor to include the update in the next computed index, and not tombstone it. Alternatively, tokens may be used to purchase unlimited server interaction for a fixed amount of time. One could imagine integrating advertisement views into a token system like this.

CONCLUSION

From the initial idea, we have developed a complex and nuanced system that may be correct. Try not to get lost in the details of Golem and instead focus on the commonalities in design and the process used. To read the full documentation created from this simple walk-though, turn to Appendix A.

Chapter 14

PAYING FOR IT

The Funding of Community Systems

INTRO

Most systems with user-generated content have issues becoming financially solvent. A social network with three users is not very social. This angst fades with growth. Once a website becomes popular, it is assured a steady following of others who join for the existing content.

Quite often the process of getting users requires the investment of venture capital. The interest behind capital is growth. If one has a system which does not have a very strong revenue stream, one is forced to cripple the implementation to find something to tax. Many systems are pushed to grow too quickly, do not get audited sufficiently, and leave many users feeling betrayed. Furthermore, it becomes hard to make choices which are better for the community than the bottom line.

THE APPCOIN ALTERNATIVE

With Bitcoin, Ethereum, Urbit, and the DAO, we have seen runaway successes with an alternative model. These systems allowed the community to fund them by buying parts of the network. These are truly trustless distributed systems. As such, it is possible to sell parts of the networks' decision-making power directly without the legal frameworks used in current investment arrangements.

All of these systems have an internal currency paid as a reward to the peers providing the service and used to buy service from the network. As a currency, the value is determined by what people are willing to pay for the service. This comes from the power that the network affords. When there are few users, the currency is almost worthless. Therefore buying currency is a bet that the network can grow. Rather than needing to sell shares of the company controlling the system (for which there is none), it is possible to sell portions of the network to gain the funding to develop and profit from the network.

It's worth noting that as the system is resilient against tampering by the creators of the system, this kind of thing only truly works at the launch of the product. While state transitions must be legal once the system has been launched, the initial state can favor certain peers if the cluster agrees on it. There are exceptions to this, though.

The first is whether there is an agreement between peers to allow for network favors to be bought. If the network wishes to strongly reward the software creator, they might agree to certain kinds of interpretations of messages. If the cluster comes to a consensus, then they decide what the protocol is. It's easy to imagine someone selling BitTorrent ratio changes, Tor priority routing to a token-holder, or something of the sort. Note that this should be thoroughly examined as a source of bugs.

If the reward is something that is paid out to those providing the service, then it is possible to simply make the global supply of that reward fixed per time-period. As the network grows, the value of a unit of currency will grow. This means that early investment of effort rewards one more than investment when it is large. Those who believe in the network can be motivated to contribute early. While this probably won't cut the developer's paycheck, it does offer a simple way to pre-profit. If the reward is higher when the network is smaller, a developer could just earn rewards in secrecy while they are the only ones in the network.

In the end, the goal is to keep the value of being in the network high enough to be attractive. If the value gained by contributing to the network is large while the network is small, then a network can bootstrap itself without investor support. Once bootstrapped, the countable value of contribution decreases but the value of the reward for contribution gets much larger. This ensures that the system remains profitable as long as it exhibits technical excellence.

ETHICS

A word of warning is due. A lot of systems believe that white lies and misinformation are harmless to disseminate. They reason that initial releases are simply technical demos to raise money for further growth. The reality of the situation is that some of this is wrong, and some of it is illegal.

When one sells promises for money, there are procedures one must go through. On one side, the government may demand one does things to avoid being liable for money laundering, gambling, or some other crime. On the other hand, personal lawsuits from people who read one documented detail when buying and found it false later may easily bankrupt a person. Worries that a distributed system sidesteps may still be bothersome during the initial sale.

If a fledgling system chooses to use unethical business means to generate hype, they are unlikely to come out unscathed. On the other hand, there is a long history of honorable companies coming out ahead.

RESOURCES

https://sale.urbit.org/

https://medium.com/the-coinbase-blog/app-coins-and-the-dawn-of-the-decentralized-business-model-8b8c951e734f

Chapter 15

CONCLUSION

A Few final Words

One may well ask: "How can you advocate breaking some laws and obeying others?" The answer lies in the fact that there are two types of laws: just and unjust. I would be the first to advocate obeying just laws. One has not only a legal but a moral responsibility to obey just laws. Conversely, one has a moral responsibility to disobey unjust laws. I would agree with St. Augustine that "an unjust law is no law at all."

"Letter from Birmingham jail" by Martin Luther King Jr.

The reader has to have noticed by now that each and every system covered here has a degree of controversy associated with it. Any technology that is powerful enough to protect a user from a foreign despot is going to be powerful enough to protect a teenager from the local police. For these reasons, cryptography has become known as an enemy to the powers that be. Many of them would have one believe that the only use of cryptography is for criminal enterprises.

I hope that in reading about the implementation of these systems, the reader has been convinced that there is a need for these types of systems. Furthermore, it should be clear that they are simply impossible without access to strong encryption. When a utility belongs to the public, it should not have a means for abuse by anybody who knows a password. It should not rely on any single person to keep track of the system's state and to mediate communication. It should be a volunteer network which provides anonymous, secure services to anybody. It should be run by the public in a manner that does not require the introduction of physical force and legal pressure to remain operational.

This field of mathematics and Computer Science is going to become very controversial in any place where the government wants to seize more control of the populace than the populace would democratically give. We've seen concerted attacks on these networks. Sites will categorically block Tor traffic. ISPs have tried to profile BitTorrent users. Attempted denial of service attacks continue against some networks without pause.

The powers that be would have one believe that this is all to return to a status quo that the internet has threatened. They would have one believe that from the edifice of public life these darkened corners of the internet have been forged. Anonymity, P2P content distribution, and anonymous payments have all been made out to be the coming of a new lawless land.

The truth is that in modern times we have seen a vast expansion of the government's powers in ways that our forefathers never thought possible. In the transition from anonymous cash and conversation to a continually audited life, a citizen has never been more watched. Systems of surveillance have become ubiquitous. By placing the revenue source for the internet primarily in advertising, the gatekeepers to the public internet have incentivized themselves to spy on the public as much as they can get away with.

Furthermore, private companies have tried to make it illegal for consumers to use their computers in ways that prevent those companies from turning a profit. Rather than running the cryptographic arms race, these companies turn to colluding with governments. Copyright terms are lengthened and the sphere of media evaluation becomes more and more privatized under a handful of companies. The public domain is under threat, putting the icons of our shared culture under lock and key.

However you feel about any of the scenarios described above, they have a number of things in common. Immediately apparent is that a small group of people hold power over a great number of people because the small group controls a service essential to public life. This power makes it possible for them to profit from abusing the trust placed in them. If we need to trust every server we interact with, we are doomed. To assault the public's access to cryptography is to assault the public's ability to trust one another without using these gatekeepers. Furthermore, without the ability to break a law, it is impossible to conduct civil disobedience and engage in anonymous political discourse. If Rosa Parks lacked the very ability to proclaim where on the bus she would remain sitting, the protest would have been impossible.

At the end of the day, the systems described in this book are hated not because they are evil. They are neither good nor evil. They are hated because they are powerful tools during bad times. Do not doubt that bad times may come. When they do, those who cannot protect themselves will be vulnerable. When any actor has the option to betray the public's trust in order to gain immense control over them, they might.

This is where your duty begins. By making sure that those who are vulnerable in your life are familiar with the means to protect themselves, you are protecting them from harm. Furthermore, you are protecting those in power from the temptation to betray the public.

THE GOLEM PROTOCOL PROPOSAL

ARCHITECTURE

Let's contrast a query under Golem to a query with a standard MVC website backend.

Standard Backend Dataflow:

1. Users query DNS to find a request-responding server behind an endpoint (usually through a load-balancer) and send the API request with arguments to the work server.

2. This work server can contact other work servers in the cluster, as well as database servers. The can make IO at any point during execution, though database manipulation is typically within a transaction. These servers will validate the input and will use it to craft these database updates.

3. These servers will all manipulate a database, relying on indexes for performance.

4. The user has no access to the database.

5. User gets back a response from their endpoint request.

6. A system looks at the database periodically and creates structures to allow the maintainer to query "business information" out of.

Golem turns the MVC app inside out by making the client the intermediary between the application servers and the database.

In Golem

1. The user queries a cluster for the last version of a document from the maintainer describing the endpoint structure.

2. The user interacts with the database before contacting the work server. They already know the data the endpoint needs to view, and they pass the

data to the endpoint after fetching it. Subsequent queries can replay this fetched data.

3. The user looks at their endpoint structure to see which primitive values (Strings, Integers, etc.) must be seen at the same time. These can be for reasons of string comparison, concatenation, predicates, etc. If the data needs to be seen in multiple places, these are considered different observation points. The user counts the number of observation points and chooses a server for each. No server appears twice, and the client maximizes geographic distribution of requests. The user uses the public key in the published document to sign a document containing a decryption key and an encryption key. The decryption key for the server is used by the client to encrypt the observation point. This document prevents the work server from needing to keep track of keys, and removes a need for an unbounded number of negotiation requests.

4. The user sends the request document and database information to a server not chosen yet. This server can see data structures tracking encrypted mini-blobs of data.

5. Work servers validate that the fetched data was inserted before the last database synchronization point by validating the location of its hash in the global Merkle tree.

6. Work servers send fragments of the input to the servers chosen for each function to service, and get

a response from them. From the responses, the return value is crafted. Database updates are threaded through in a single transaction.

7. The client examines the database updates to see if the work servers stored information in the updates that they are not alright with. If they consent to the data storage, they push the updates to the keys they control, along with the verification that the data followed a valid path through the program.

The above summary sped through a lot of implementation details, but gives the reader an idea of how the data flows through the system and some of the logic behind the architecture. We will turn to the data structures of the system next, as they dictate the operations of the system.

DATA STRUCTURES

The database model that we present is based on the Kappa Architecture (http://milinda.pathirage.org/kappa-architecture.com/).

The Kappa Architecture is a view of databases which arose from the rise of the distributed log. In distributed systems such as databases, we find that a sane cache eviction policy and cluster consistency are difficult to extract from an existing database. As more and more clusters turn to the use of a distributed log for synchronization, its application to databases becomes more attractive. The idea behind the Kappa Architecture is to insert all modifications into a shared log and to create a database by traversing the log from start to finish and executing updates. In this way, the database is a temporary cache of the real data store. Updates can be dropped and the index can be rebuilt, giving the database a lot of flexibility.

Right now, let's focus on the actual structure of the database. As we said above, the database is a log. Queries are made from the "index" structures which are created by traversing the update log. This means that all we have to do is to offer a distributed log, right? Not so fast. We don't want everybody appending to the same log, as this allows clients to interfere with one another. Each client has one log per piece of relevant data, and the program maintainer is responsible for providing snapshots and for creating the indices that the rest of the cluster uses.

Our append-only logs are quite simple. We chose to use the Bitcoin blockchain and the BitTorrent swarm as the database. A user can create a transaction including OP_RETURN, which allows them to embed information in the blockchain. This creates a nice linear ordering to updates globally. The embedded information includes the hash of a torrent containing the insertion commands to enter into the log.

Finding the newest version of a value at a key then becomes finding the last transaction from a given Bitcoin address, and fetching the torrent. This has latency, but clients should never have to query their stream directly. Instead, the Supervisor-made indices exist for primary database querying.

The question is still begged; how do we know that the data in our database is consistent. Can we afford to trust anyone? By using what I've termed a "prime stamp," the supervisor of the system can ensure that transactions only occur along the paths that the codebase would at first.

Prime stamps work because modulo is cheap but prime factorization is hard. Every transaction-verification window, all updates in the database are given a large prime to tag it. When a server adds an update to the updates for the client to insert into the database, they multiply a "state" number by the prime they're responsible for. They also sign the number with their private key.

This state is threaded through all requests. The client picks a random number and sends it to the endpoint. From there on out, the servers thread this random number through and multiply it by large primes. The client puts this accumulated stamp into a transaction block in a torrent that is pushed to each Bitcoin "stream" which has a key which is modified by the transaction.

If a transaction stamp divides the accumulation, then the request was crafted by the servers with very high probability. The thing though is that these stamps are only published after a time-period snapshot is taken. That means that an attacker would need to do statistical profiling of many updates made from clients which hit the same endpoint, and find the GCD of these primes. Now not all servers doing the same update will necessarily have the same prime tag. Duplication and versioning allows for a lot of code path obfuscation. The attacker needs to try the permutation of the primes found.

How many times can an attacker get feedback on a prime stamp being right? Well, they can only get it wrong once. And when they do, they lose the proof-of-work necessary for a server to get an identity and to get trusted with code. It's also worth noting that this factoring and guessing must be done during a single time cycle. At a very small scale, the problem still becomes infeasible when the cycle time is less than a half hour or so.

PROTOCOL

Terminology

Blockchain – The Bitcoin blockchain

Supervisor – The agent running the service, foots the server's costs

Server – The agent hosting code for one or more Applications

Client – The agent being serviced by the Supervisor's application code, running on numerous Servers

Prime stamp – A product of primes representing a database transaction.

Supervisor Bootstraps Application

1.   Supervisor generates a master public/private key pair and a secondary public/private key pair. They use the master key pair to sign a certificate chain for the secondary key pair. This allows the supervisor to place the secondary key pair on a quasi-untrusted server, and to use the master key pair to revoke or grant this and future secondary keys.

2.   Supervisor takes program description (described below), and posts a job offer document to the blockchain containing a type tag and a torrent hash of the offer. The offer contains specifics like the pay rate per request, the minimum number of servers needed to start serving, the BitTorrent tracker, and the expected client and server proof-of-work difficulties (to prevent denial of service).

3.   Supervisor waits until a sufficient number of servers have agreed to participate in the same half-hour time window.

4.   Supervisor begins the "Tick" action until the number of servers drops too low.

5.   If the Supervisor wishes to update the code, they will post a new job bid which references the previous one and wait until the next "Tick" for things to propagate.

Server Joins Application

1.   Server sees the job offer document type on the blockchain, and fetch the torrent

2.   Server decides to accept job

3.   Server does Proof-of-Work to create document accepting work. This is their identity certificate. It includes a public key and an available hostname and port to access them on.

4.   Server posts data to a torrent, puts hash in the blockchain. Server sends Supervisor smallest possible transaction.

5.   Server and Supervisor begin a micro-transaction.

Client Reserves Database Key

1.   Client picks a new Bitcoin address and pushes a commit with an initial value for the value held there.

2.   The client then refers to this new Bitcoin address in a transaction from the address used to register the Client. This includes the type tag of the data stored here. Datatypes must be types listed in the endpoint specification.

3.   The client public key is the only key that can write to it.

Client Makes Endpoint Request

1.   Client uses Tick document, examines endpoint request to find out the arguments to pass to the endpoint, and how many different servers are necessary to service it.

2.   If endpoint needs a database query to work on, Client uses the Supervisor's index to find the data necessary to service.

3.   Client uses Tick document, finds a server for each entry-point hash in the document. For each server, client generates two symmetric keys and encrypts them both with the public key of the server. They then encrypt the data that only this server can see. This prevents the need for key negotiation to happen in the middle of servicing a request.

1.　　　Client picks a "top-level" server with the endpoint's hash, one which won't be able to see any primitives, and encrypts the entire message with public key for this server.

2.　　　Client does proof-of-work for request.

5.　　　Client sends the entire payload to the "top-level" server and waits for a response.

6.　　　Client vets the server updates to make for information leakage.

7.　　　Client inserts updates into keys by posting torrent of diff of updates and inserting hash into blockchain.

Supervisor Tick

　　　　The tick contains data for the last cycle as well as for the next 3 "tick" cycles. We have the 3-cycle delay because this gives the servers the time to get the next cycle loaded. It's cheap to offer the buffer here. It's worth noting that as this is a torrent file, servers and clients can download individual files out of it. For this reason, many of the fields below are separate files in the torrent.

Summary Portion

1.　　　Examine the blockchain for update hashes pushed by tracked client addresses.

2.　　　Concatenate these blocks together and embed into document.

3.　　　Rebuild indexes from data changes and embed into document. This is important because while the logs would be $O(N)$ to traverse on every read, we can create many cached index structures to amortize update costs.

4.　　　Post the collection of transaction stamps valid during this time period. It's vital to post this while hashing the current values, or clients could retroactively use the stamps.

5.　　　Receive server logs, and pay server via micro-transaction for work done.

Next Portion

1.　　　Check that the minimum number of servers posted in the contract have been offered. If not, sleep for time cycle.

2.　　　Check if clients have sent any transactions signed by servers that are not accepted transactions. Use known primes for that cycle to check the factorization of the transaction, O(N) in terms of number of mutations. Can do SIMD. Use the signature order to find out first who didn't add the prime they should have, and eject them from the cluster by placing a "tombstone" in the blockchain for their previous server proof-of-work.

3.   Check the gossip documents sent, see if servers have been below latency promised latency for a fraction of last few cycles. If so, cancel contract. Require a number of cycles before giving them another chance. Exponential back off on chances.

4.   Find and shuffle primes for each database mutation call site

5.   For each transaction control flow that's acceptable, compute the prime stamp with the new primes.

6.   Shuffle and probabilistically duplicate and version endpoint functions, and distribute to nodes.

7.   Encrypt each for each server and append code with "tick" time for it to run (3 in future). Each endpoint code is a separate file in the torrent.

8.   Append schema with documentation -> endpoint message, including the primitive encryption that has to be done for each endpoint. In this way, the API is self-documenting.

Lastly, sign this document and push to BitTorrent, put hash on blockchain.

Server Response to Tick

1.   Replace last set of code and prime keys with new set

2.   Fetch next 3-offset set of code and keys and prepare.

3.   Encrypt list of client interaction receipts with Supervisor's public key and place in torrent. Send hash of torrent to Supervisor in exchange for a microtransaction update to the new owed balance.

Client Response to Tick

1.   Validate that all commits made were not poisoned by servers. If so, notify Supervisor. This can be done lazily, on the next query.

ATTACKS

There are not many attack options available to any actors here. All would amount to a punishable violation of trust with no lasting impact beyond loss of peers.

If the client tries to insert data into the database without using the application to create the transactions, then the servers will not have signed the transactions and created the stamp. This kind of bad behavior is easy to spot. We will destroy the client's identity with the system. Proof-of-work makes this attack unfeasible; the attacker will do much more work than anybody else.

If a server returns an incorrect set of transactions, we know. If a server wants to eavesdrop on users, they don't have access to enough information to learn more than a small set of primitives. Furthermore, the fact that the client chooses the servers means that an attacker would have to control most of the network to see more than one chunk of primitives.

Denial of service is countered by the pervasive rate limiting that proof-of-work and the blockchain brings.

Lastly, what if a server knew the transaction stamps and forged a bad transaction? Well what would this entail? They can't use the already-released transaction stamps, as they're out of date. They'd need to control enough servers to understand all of the control flow and see all of the tags. The ability of clients to enforce geographic distribution means that seizing enough computers rapidly enough is unfeasible.

CODE SPECIFICATION

In order for our system to be usable, a specific interface has to be presented to the application developer. If we allowed for arbitrary looping, it would be possible for functions to route to each other such that the cluster would loop indefinitely. Rather than take on the halting problem through heuristics, a more principled approach is to ban unrestricted looping entirely.

Wait, you say, how can I do useful work without looping? While we are reducing the number of total applications that can be written in theory, we are not reducing the number of useful applications in practice. The application servers shouldn't be making IO requests to the world, that would be a design which makes subverting the Golem system trivial. Instead, the IO is carried out by the clients and the database values and request data are sent to the servers.

The servers are a purely functional mapping of finite, pre-parsed data structures into finite data structures. There is no need to introduce arbitrarily diverging computation into the system. Instead, we will expose the primitives of map, filter, and fold while banning iteration keywords and both recursion and mutual recursion. The functional programming idea of a zipper extends these to trees. With trees, we gain key-value stores. The primitives are therefore sufficiently flexible for reasonable programs, and allow us to analyze them tractably.

Rather than writing a new language myself, we will lay out a design for an ORM-like library which can build these programs up. By using opaque types for "Golem values," the functions can build up programs through working with values as if they were database objects. The program written by the developer is actually ran once, on the developer's machine. There is nothing hiding in unexecuted conditionals: all Golem conditional statements are executed because they are essentially code generation functions. This program outputs a JSON document specifying the Golem program created. The time daemon will accept this program and will carry out the supervisor's roles.

Consider a function that receives endpoint requests. The argument to this request is a JSON object which contains primitive (String, Integer, etc.) values, and nested JSON dictionaries. The program that the developer takes will register these endpoint functions. In this way, the request object is "injected" into the function. We exploit this inversion of control to pass a JSON object which has the same structure as the expected format, but passes "opaque types" in the place of primitives.

In order to see the value in an opaque type, one must pass it a callback. This is where the program jumps to another server. As JavaScript is fairly used to callback-driven workflows, there are many libraries to present syntactic sugar here. These callbacks build a value that is of an opaque type. This return value will look like the value returned to the API consumer but something far weirder is actually happening here. Each opaque type is really a reference to the end of linked list of updates to the initial value it has. As the opaque types combine, the lists simply interleave. The return value of the endpoint function is thus a dataflow log of how the output is yielded from the input.

At points, the functions will make database queries. These queries are executed at "compile-time". We can therefore track messages sent to the database library, and build up an ordering of queries to insert into every update log. This visibility allows us to "hoist" all queries to the top of an entry-point block. Updates append to the update log, which are returned to the client.

In the case where queries require generated values, we will notify the developer at compile-time that we had to split the function. This does mean more state visibility, but this is only a problem when the application wants to hide database access. This privilege is an anti-pattern that we've explicitly negated in the design of Golem.

After arriving at a dataflow representation of the program, the wire format becomes a series of calls and statements to make to yield the arguments for the eventual data constructor returned to the person hitting the endpoint, along with the update log.

PREVIOUS WORK

The core of the idea comes from onion routing. Nobody can see enough of the entire global state to understand enough to do harm. By the time information is obtainable, it is too late for it to be useful. The fact that obfuscation can truly work when one has safety in numbers led to the architecture of the application server cluster.

I was also inspired by https://github.com/elendirx/web2web . The method of using the blockchain as a carrier for an individual stream of updates, and using that to serve BitTorrent hashes, proved instrumental to the ability to host coordination documents in a verifiable way.

IMPLEMENTATION DIFFICULTY

The infrastructure for Server execution is really limited to an interpreter of map, filter, and fold structured recursion, as well as pattern matching on data constructors and creating them. This would be an undertaking for a new language, but since this is a high-level library we manage to elide most of the issues. Something that would be fun to play with one day is using Tensorflow as the execution framework. Tensorflow is a dataflow execution framework and offers both the needed primitives and the ability to dynamically optimize around actual control flow. A JIT which specializes on executed Golem function will definitely help with the costs of interpretation, as endpoints have an enforced structure.

The Client work is really just a combination of off-the-shelf parts. Web2web shows that WebTorrent and blockchain scraping is fairly trivial to implement with the existing libraries. The only thing that remains is to create a wrapper around the database fetching and the server selection for the query. This logic is fairly uniform, so there shouldn't be much cyclomatic complexity here.

The Supervisor daemon will be the largest amount of labor, but is limited to the summary document creation, the prime-stamp logic, seeding of torrents necessary to the application, and code transformation. The code transformation should be fairly easy to work with since we are really just creating a logging library that looks like an ORM.

CONCLUSION

I believe that Golem represents a fairly significant contribution to the problem of trust in website hosting and administration. By treating an application as a conversation between the client and the code author, we are able to use the servers as an untrusted third party. The code author defines the legal application states, and the swarm of clients and servers work to ensure that the database only contains data generated by valid transactions. The history of database transactions is used to create a performant, indexed data structure for clients to read from.

It's worthwhile to consider the multitude of recent crimes and coercions that would have been unable to occur in this system. Hackers have very little to hack. If they hack a server, all they can do is get the server ejected from the cluster. If they hack a client, all they can do is impersonate the client; this is an attack that is outside of our scope. If the hack a supervisor, the supervisor can revoke the secondary key pair and user the master key to re-assert a valid index structure and cluster code distribution. The only program state that really exists is the append-only log of commits from the clients. Everything else is a constructed view of the data that can be re-created when necessary. State can't be lost, and there is no state to really steal since the non-persistent data is distributed throughout the entire cluster.

By trusting nothing beyond the difficulty of prime factorization, we have created a system in which trust cannot be stolen or abused to do lasting harm. That is an Internet that I'd like to be a citizen of.

COPYRIGHT

1. Definitions

a. "Adaptation" means a work based upon the Work, or upon the Work and other pre-existing works, such as a translation, adaptation, derivative work, arrangement of music or other alterations of a literary or artistic work, or phonogram or performance and includes cinematographic adaptations or any other form in which the Work may be recast, transformed, or adapted including in any form recognizably derived from the original, except that a work that constitutes a Collection will not be considered an Adaptation for the purpose of this License. For the avoidance of doubt, where the Work is a musical work, performance or phonogram, the synchronization of the Work in timed-relation with a moving image ("synching") will be considered an Adaptation for the purpose of this License.

b. "Collection" means a collection of literary or artistic works, such as encyclopedias and anthologies, or performances, phonograms or broadcasts, or other works or subject matter other than works listed

in Section 1 (f) below, which, by reason of the selection and

arrangement of their contents, constitute intellectual creations, in

which the Work is included in its entirety in unmodified form along

with one or more other contributions, each constituting separate and

independent works in themselves, which together are assembled into a

collective whole. A work that constitutes a Collection will not be

considered an Adaptation (as defined above) for the purposes of this

License.

c. *"Distribute" means to make available to the public the original and*

copies of the Work or Adaptation, as appropriate, through sale or

other transfer of ownership.

d. *"Licensor" means the individual, individuals, entity or entities that*

offer(s) the Work under the terms of this License.

e. *"Original Author" means, in the case of a literary or artistic work,*

the individual, individuals, entity or entities who created the Work

or if no individual or entity can be identified, the publisher; and in

addition (i) in the case of a performance the actors, singers,

musicians, dancers, and other persons who act, sing, deliver, declaim,

play in, interpret or otherwise perform literary or artistic works or

expressions of folklore; (ii) in the case of a phonogram the producer

being the person or legal entity who first fixes the sounds of a

performance or other sounds; and, (iii) in the case of broadcasts, the

organization that transmits the broadcast.

f. *"Work" means the literary and/or artistic work offered under the terms*

of this License including without limitation any production in the literary, scientific and artistic domain, whatever may be the mode or

form of its expression including digital form, such as a book,

pamphlet and other writing; a lecture, address, sermon or other work

of the same nature; a dramatic or dramatico-musical work; a

choreographic work or entertainment in dumb show; a musical

composition with or without words; a cinematographic work to which are

assimilated works expressed by a process analogous to cinematography;

a work of drawing, painting, architecture, sculpture, engraving or

lithography; a photographic work to which are assimilated works

expressed by a process analogous to photography; a work of applied

art; an illustration, map, plan, sketch or three-dimensional work

relative to geography, topography, architecture or science; a

performance; a broadcast; a phonogram; a compilation of data to the

extent it is protected as a copyrightable work; or a work performed by

a variety or circus performer to the extent it is not otherwise

considered a literary or artistic work.

g. "You" means an individual or entity exercising rights under this

License who has not previously violated the terms of this License with

respect to the Work, or who has received express permission from the

Licensor to exercise rights under this License despite a previous

violation.

h. "Publicly Perform" means to perform public recitations of the Work and

to communicate to the public those public recitations, by any means or

process, including by wire or wireless means or public digital

performances; to make available to the public Works in such a way that

members of the public may access these Works from a place and at a place individually chosen by them; to perform the Work to the public by any means or process and the communication to the public of the performances of the Work, including by public digital performance; to broadcast and rebroadcast the Work by any means including signs, sounds or images.

i. "Reproduce" means to make copies of the Work by any means including without limitation by sound or visual recordings and the right of fixation and reproducing fixations of the Work, including storage of a protected performance or phonogram in digital form or other electronic medium.

2. Fair Dealing Rights. Nothing in this License is intended to reduce, limit, or restrict any uses free from copyright or rights arising from limitations or exceptions that are provided for in connection with the copyright protection under copyright law or other applicable laws.

3. License Grant. Subject to the terms and conditions of this License, Licensor hereby grants You a worldwide, royalty-free, non-exclusive, perpetual (for the duration of the applicable copyright) license to exercise the rights in the Work as stated below:

a. to Reproduce the Work, to incorporate the Work into one or more Collections, and to Reproduce the Work as incorporated in the Collections;

b. to create and Reproduce Adaptations provided that any such Adaptation, including any translation in any medium, takes reasonable steps to *clearly label, demarcate or otherwise identify that changes were made*

to the original Work. For example, a translation could be marked "The

original work was translated from English to Spanish," or a

modification could indicate "The original work has been modified.";

c. to Distribute and Publicly Perform the Work including as incorporated

in Collections; and,

d. to Distribute and Publicly Perform Adaptations.

e. For the avoidance of doubt:

i. Non-waivable Compulsory License Schemes. In those jurisdictions in

which the right to collect royalties through any statutory or

compulsory licensing scheme cannot be waived, the Licensor

reserves the exclusive right to collect such royalties for any

exercise by You of the rights granted under this License;

ii. Waivable Compulsory License Schemes. In those jurisdictions in

which the right to collect royalties through any statutory or

compulsory licensing scheme can be waived, the Licensor waives the

exclusive right to collect such royalties for any exercise by You

of the rights granted under this License; and,

iii. Voluntary License Schemes. The Licensor waives the right to

collect royalties, whether individually or, in the event that the

Licensor is a member of a collecting society that administers

voluntary licensing schemes, via that society, from any exercise

by You of the rights granted under this License.

The above rights may be exercised in all media and formats whether now known or hereafter devised. The above rights include the right to make such modifications as are technically necessary to exercise the rights in other media and formats. Subject to Section 8(f), all rights not expressly granted by Licensor are hereby reserved.

4. Restrictions. The license granted in Section 3 above is expressly made subject to and limited by the following restrictions:

a. You may Distribute or Publicly Perform the Work only under the terms of this License. You must include a copy of, or the Uniform Resource Identifier (URI) for, this License with every copy of the Work You Distribute or Publicly Perform. You may not offer or impose any terms on the Work that restrict the terms of this License or the ability of the recipient of the Work to exercise the rights granted to that recipient under the terms of the License. You may not sublicense the Work. You must keep intact all notices that refer to this License and to the disclaimer of warranties with every copy of the Work You Distribute or Publicly Perform. When You Distribute or Publicly Perform the Work, You may not impose any effective technological measures on the Work that restrict the ability of a recipient of the Work from You to exercise the rights granted to that recipient under the terms of the License. This Section 4(a) applies to the Work as incorporated in a Collection, but this does not require the Collection apart from the Work itself to be made subject to the terms of this License. If You create a Collection, upon notice from any Licensor You must, to the extent practicable, remove from the Collection any credit *as required by Section 4(b), as requested. If You create an*

Adaptation, upon notice from any Licensor You must, to the extent

practicable, remove from the Adaptation any credit as required by

Section 4(b), as requested.

b. *If You Distribute, or Publicly Perform the Work or any Adaptations or*

Collections, You must, unless a request has been made pursuant to

Section 4(a), keep intact all copyright notices for the Work and

provide, reasonable to the medium or means You are utilizing: (i) the

name of the Original Author (or pseudonym, if applicable) if supplied,

and/or if the Original Author and/or Licensor designate another party

or parties (e.g., a sponsor institute, publishing entity, journal) for

attribution ("Attribution Parties") in Licensor's copyright notice,

terms of service or by other reasonable means, the name of such party

or parties; (ii) the title of the Work if supplied; (iii) to the

extent reasonably practicable, the URI, if any, that Licensor

specifies to be associated with the Work, unless such URI does not

refer to the copyright notice or licensing information for the Work;

and (iv) , consistent with Section 3(b), in the case of an Adaptation,

a credit identifying the use of the Work in the Adaptation (e.g.,

"French translation of the Work by Original Author," or "Screenplay

based on original Work by Original Author"). The credit required by

this Section 4 (b) may be implemented in any reasonable manner;

provided, however, that in the case of a Adaptation or Collection, at

a minimum such credit will appear, if a credit for all contributing

authors of the Adaptation or Collection appears, then as part of these

credits and in a manner at least as prominent as the credits for the

231

other contributing authors. For the avoidance of doubt, You may only use the credit required by this Section for the purpose of attribution in the manner set out above and, by exercising Your rights under this License, You may not implicitly or explicitly assert or imply any connection with, sponsorship or endorsement by the Original Author, Licensor and/or Attribution Parties, as appropriate, of You or Your use of the Work, without the separate, express prior written permission of the Original Author, Licensor and/or Attribution Parties.

c. Except as otherwise agreed in writing by the Licensor or as may be otherwise permitted by applicable law, if You Reproduce, Distribute or Publicly Perform the Work either by itself or as part of any Adaptations or Collections, You must not distort, mutilate, modify or take other derogatory action in relation to the Work which would be prejudicial to the Original Author's honor or reputation. Licensor agrees that in those jurisdictions (e.g. Japan), in which any exercise of the right granted in Section 3(b) of this License (the right to make Adaptations) would be deemed to be a distortion, mutilation, modification or other derogatory action prejudicial to the Original Author's honor and reputation, the Licensor will waive or not assert, as appropriate, this Section, to the fullest extent permitted by the applicable national law, to enable You to reasonably exercise Your right under Section 3(b) of this License (right to make Adaptations) but not otherwise.

5. Representations, Warranties and Disclaimer

UNLESS OTHERWISE MUTUALLY AGREED TO BY THE PARTIES IN WRITING,
LICENSOR

OFFERS THE WORK AS-IS AND MAKES NO REPRESENTATIONS OR WARRANTIES
OF ANY

KIND CONCERNING THE WORK, EXPRESS, IMPLIED, STATUTORY OR OTHERWISE,

INCLUDING, WITHOUT LIMITATION, WARRANTIES OF TITLE, MERCHANTIBILITY,

FITNESS FOR A PARTICULAR PURPOSE, NONINFRINGEMENT, OR THE ABSENCE OF

LATENT OR OTHER DEFECTS, ACCURACY, OR THE PRESENCE OF ABSENCE OF
ERRORS,

WHETHER OR NOT DISCOVERABLE. SOME JURISDICTIONS DO NOT ALLOW THE
EXCLUSION

OF IMPLIED WARRANTIES, SO SUCH EXCLUSION MAY NOT APPLY TO YOU.

6. Limitation on Liability. EXCEPT TO THE EXTENT REQUIRED BY APPLICABLE

LAW, IN NO EVENT WILL LICENSOR BE LIABLE TO YOU ON ANY LEGAL THEORY
FOR

ANY SPECIAL, INCIDENTAL, CONSEQUENTIAL, PUNITIVE OR EXEMPLARY
DAMAGES

ARISING OUT OF THIS LICENSE OR THE USE OF THE WORK, EVEN IF LICENSOR
HAS

BEEN ADVISED OF THE POSSIBILITY OF SUCH DAMAGES.

7. Termination

a. This License and the rights granted hereunder will terminate

automatically upon any breach by You of the terms of this License.

Individuals or entities who have received Adaptations or Collections

from You under this License, however, will not have their licenses

terminated provided such individuals or entities remain in full compliance with those licenses. Sections 1, 2, 5, 6, 7, and 8 will

survive any termination of this License.

b. Subject to the above terms and conditions, the license granted here is

perpetual (for the duration of the applicable copyright in the Work).

Notwithstanding the above, Licensor reserves the right to release the

Work under different license terms or to stop distributing the Work at

any time; provided, however that any such election will not serve to

withdraw this License (or any other license that has been, or is

required to be, granted under the terms of this License), and this

License will continue in full force and effect unless terminated as

stated above.

8. Miscellaneous

a. Each time You Distribute or Publicly Perform the Work or a Collection,

the Licensor offers to the recipient a license to the Work on the same

terms and conditions as the license granted to You under this License.

b. Each time You Distribute or Publicly Perform an Adaptation, Licensor

offers to the recipient a license to the original Work on the same

terms and conditions as the license granted to You under this License.

c. If any provision of this License is invalid or unenforceable under

applicable law, it shall not affect the validity or enforceability of

the remainder of the terms of this License, and without further action

by the parties to this agreement, such provision shall be reformed to

the minimum extent necessary to make such provision valid and

enforceable.

d. No term or provision of this License shall be deemed waived and no
  breach consented to unless such waiver or consent shall be in writing
  and signed by the party to be charged with such waiver or consent.

e. This License constitutes the entire agreement between the parties with
  respect to the Work licensed here. There are no understandings,
  agreements or representations with respect to the Work not specified
  here. Licensor shall not be bound by any additional provisions that
  may appear in any communication from You. This License may not be
  modified without the mutual written agreement of the Licensor and You.

f. The rights granted under, and the subject matter referenced, in this
  License were drafted utilizing the terminology of the Berne Convention
  for the Protection of Literary and Artistic Works (as amended on
  September 28, 1979), the Rome Convention of 1961, the WIPO Copyright
  Treaty of 1996, the WIPO Performances and Phonograms Treaty of 1996
  and the Universal Copyright Convention (as revised on July 24, 1971).
  These rights and subject matter take effect in the relevant
  jurisdiction in which the License terms are sought to be enforced
  according to the corresponding provisions of the implementation of
  those treaty provisions in the applicable national law. If the
  standard suite of rights granted under applicable copyright law
  includes additional rights not granted under this License, such
  additional rights are deemed to be included in the License; this
  License is not intended to restrict the license of any rights under
  applicable law.

www.ingramcontent.com/pod-product-compliance
Lightning Source LLC
Chambersburg PA
CBHW031837170526
45157CB00001B/334